On Human Being

Olivier Clément

On Human Being
a spiritual anthropology

Foreword by
George A. Maloney

New City Press

New York London Manila

First Published in French as
Questions sur l'homme
by Editions Anne Sigier, Sainte-Foy, 1986

Published in English:
In Great Britain by
New City
57 Twyford Avenue
London W3 9PZ

In the United States of America by
New City Press
202 Cardinal Road
Hyde Park NY 12538
www.newcitypress.com

Translated by
Jeremy Hummerstone

Cover Picture by
G. Viviani

Cover Design by
Tomeu Mayans

A catalogue record for this book is available
from the British library

ISBN
UK edition: 0- 904287- 72- 6
USA edition: 1- 56548 -143- 7

Typeset in Great Britain by
New City, London

Printed in Canada

Contents

Foreword

I have often been struck when the theologian Yves Congar is quoted by John Paul II in saying that Christians today must breathe with two lungs: the spirituality of the Christian West and that of the East. Would you not agree with me that most Christians in the West have little knowledge of the more ancient and most valid traditions that link us to the first 'one, holy and apostolic Church' of the early followers of Christ?

The well-known Orthodox author and professor of Eastern Christian spirituality in Paris, Olivier Clément, offers us here an extremely important book. It should challenge both Orthodox and other Christians in the West not only to be open to the treasures of the traditions of the Christian East of old but, above all, to receive these traditions, expressed here in modern, existential terms, and through them enrich and revitalize the Churches at the dawn of a new millennium and into the 21st century.

Perhaps from a deeper study of patristic theology, especially the theological anthropology of the Eastern Fathers, Western theology can regain something of its existential dynamism and theology will again become a 'life in God-Trinity'. In turn, Eastern theologians and lay people may profit from the Western view of social consciousness that opens up Eastern mystical prayer to a universal compassion for all peoples in need throughout the world. Thus, a work on a geo-global level would evolve and develop the cosmos in all of its materiality so as to allow the Logos made flesh to transform all of the creation into the body of Christ.

Some Catholic readers might be perplexed by the author's writing out of the ancient and modern Orthodox traditions on married clergy and the Orthodox practice of granting divorces by their tradition of *oeconomia*, that is, the power of the keys of the Church. But I highly recommend this book of Clément's as the best way for us in the West to learn how to breathe not only with our Western lung but to start with our Eastern one as well.

'The glory of God is a human being fully alive', as Irenaeus of the second century wrote. Let us strive to breathe fully, so that we Christians may be one as the Father and the Son are one through the same Holy Spirit of love.

George A. Maloney

1

Anthropology: An Approach by Way of Repentance

From our own experience and from our observation of others we are aware that human nature is damaged. Damaged, first of all, within each one of us: the 'self' is a shadow theatre of neurotic characters, and it is they who are pulling our strings instead of the other way about. Our faculties are disunited and out of order. While the rational intelligence is busy making distinctions, the 'heart', in obedience to dark subconscious forces, is obliterating them. We are turned this way and that, lacking any centre of balance.

Not only are we disunited as individuals, we are the same in relation to each other. Whether we are alone or involved with others, we remain separate and hostile, alone even in our involvement.

Which is to say, in theological terms, that our condition is fallen.

In this condition it is impossible to develop a Christian anthropology. Our thinking can only lead to a dead end. If we examine the personality in its isolated state we become imprisoned in the blindness that caused our 'alienation' in the first place, an alienation which is not merely social but basic to our very existence.

The shadows, however, are shot through with flashes of light. In mad moments of love or creativity, in the transparency of a glance, or when we are suddenly overtaken by sheer wonderment at our existence, depths of enlightenment are revealed.

Humanity cannot be explained in terms of itself. The fine word
'ethos', debased by us into 'ethics', originally meant 'dwelling-
place'. And Heraclitus said, 'The dwelling-place of man is God'.

Separation, hell and death

So how do we embark on this study of humanity of which the
revelation of God is an essential part?

Not by science, as in 'social sciences', to which we shall give due
acknowledgement in passing, but by *Christian knowledge*, which
is knowledge in the context of faith, apprehended not by any particular faculty but through the whole person, knowledge which
begins and proceeds by way of repentance, or as the Gospel and
the Greek Fathers call it, *metanoia*: *the turning round* of our self-
awareness, the Copernican shift of the self (individual or collective)
from geocentric to heliocentric, enabling us to see in the depth of
everything around us the furnace of the divine sun.

But first let us attack the walls of our prison. One of the best
definitions of fallenness comes from St Andrew of Crete, a 7th century monk whose Penitential Canon is read in the Eastern Churches
at the beginning of Great Lent, the season of penitence by which
we prepare to celebrate the Resurrection. St Andrew says, 'Man is
the idolater of himself'. That impulse to worship which is basic to
human nature, human beings have diverted towards themselves,
thus cutting themselves off from the Source of life (on which nevertheless they still depend) and turning back towards the nothingness
out of which they were created. Human beings cannot actually
annihilate themselves, but they become the slave of death. And
death is not only the inexorable fact with which every human life
must end, for even in death we can see God's mercy at work. All
the while we are advancing along our destined path we are well
aware that everything must finish, that we have done too much,
and seen too much. Like the thief on the cross, we can say, 'In our
case we deserved it; we are paying for what we did' (Luke 23.41).

Much more serious is the state of death we are in even while we are alive, because it denotes a life against nature, against the longing for immortality, that compulsion to worship which is the secret truth about us. In that sense, we are in death. And we realize that our human nature and the universe around us are literally in a state of disintegration.

One of the most astonishing features of our time is the tendency of spiritual truths, till recently known only to contemplatives, to become historical facts. So the splitting of the atom is only the outward expression in history of the spiritual state of disintegration in humanity known to Tradition and called just the same thing, 'atomization'.

When the self turns away from God, it can no longer contain its nature, it becomes an individual – *atomos!* – in which the nature is broken up. While in Christ and in holy people we see human and universal nature (using 'nature' in its proper theological, not philosophical, sense) working together in perfect harmony, in our case the unity is 'atomized'.

We are side by side but our faces are closed towards each other, wearing an alien expression that cuts us off from the whole of creation. The impulse of thanksgiving in nature has become a blind force. Instead of working through us to find its fulfilment in God, it plays with our closed and misshapen selves, rattling these 'atoms' together.

And this is the condition we are in: we must kill to eat until we die and are absorbed by decayed nature; we must kill also, in one way or another, to find an ephemeral security; we seek security through mastery of the world – and it becomes our tomb. *Eros*, which ought to point towards immortality, becomes simply the means of perpetuating the species. The 'passions', as the ascetics call them, turn into idols. Nature, now become impersonal, enslaves humanity and plunges it into death.

Individuals tighten their grasp on freedom, but it is a freedom devoid of meaning, attaching itself to outward things and becoming enslaved to them and to the desire for possession which they arouse. The only thing that can put an end to this impossible and ultimately destructive love is death. Kirilov, in Dostoevsky's *The Devils*, is perfectly detached, perfectly open; when, for example, he contemplates a leaf just beginning to turn yellow in autumn, he is aware of eternity. He believes that if he were to die of his own free will at such a moment, he would achieve ultimate fulfilment, true freedom; he would be God. And at the chosen moment he kills himself. But he is not God, he is dead. There lies the root of our slavery. Every view of the world which does not include death or deliberately ignores it can only be an illusion.

So on the one hand we have individual freedom which is meaningless. On the other hand we have an impulse to worship and to celebrate, a way in to the infinite, which is the 'nature' within us; which, unless the self allows it expression, and uses it to attach us to God, turns into a senseless impersonal force, carrying us away in its momentum. It becomes a search for ecstasy – no matter of what kind – achieved through destruction, drugs or sex. The worshipful integration of nature in the person is inverted in a hellish imprisonment of the individual in nature.

It is one of the essential marks of our fallen condition that we are not only in death, but already, here and now, in hell.

The Fathers of the Church cannot help us here. Let us quote instead two short phrases of Sartre, a rigorously ascetical thinker, whose asceticism either ends in nothingness or seeks an escape in revolution for its own sake. 'Hell is other people,' he writes, and again, 'My Fall is the existence of others.' For, as he says in *Being and Nothingness*, 'The essential nature of human beings is none other than the yearning to be God. So their essential nature is inessential to them.'

The yearning to be God, the yearning for the absolute, when diverted towards the contingent, destroys it, becomes lethal. Other people are seen merely as obstacles to our achievement of communion. Even while the desire to love persists, they are reminders of our state of non-communion and its mortal outcome. As people say after committing what are rightly called crimes of passion, 'I loved her too much, I murdered her.'

In a reciprocal relationship there has to be on the one side acceptance and yielding, symbolizing the feminine, and on the other energy and force, the masculine. I say symbolizing, first because every person, man or woman, actually possesses both at once, one or the other being dominant. Also because sexuality is not merely the legitimate expression of our whole *Eros* – which can be much more fully expressed in service and friendship, artistic creativity or spiritual contemplation – but is itself symbolic. So describing reciprocal relations in terms of this sexual symbolism, we notice that the encounter between the sexes has, in this fallen world, been degraded into sadism and masochism. Similarly with the vertical dimension: our original participation, in the Spirit, in the communion of Father and Son in the Trinity – 'That they may be one as we are one,' as Christ says to the Father in St John's Gospel – has been degraded into a thousand forms of the master-slave relationship.

Such is the fallen condition of the world that the Greek Fathers speak of it in terms of defeat, disease, absence, and (a recurrent theme of this chapter) separation. The Indians call it an Illusion; one that, feeding off a creation that is wholly good, causes such endless suffering, such sighs and groans of the whole created order, that St Paul compared them to those of childbirth. And the comparison brings out not a likeness but an unlikeness, one that proliferates everywhere in monsters of bewitching beauty. The images (and imaginings) of Fellini in his *Satyricon* show how beauty, if accorded an absolute value which does not belong to it, becomes inflated and deformed.

By contrast, the God of the Gospel and mainstream Christianity neither avenges, nor terrorizes nor castrates. At the heart of the Gospel message there is nothing but Love, which is infinite, sacrificial and lifegiving, which respects our freedom 'to death, even death on the cross' (Phil. 2.8).

The greatest witnesses of patristic times, from St Irenaeus of Lyons to St Gregory of Nyssa and St Maximus the Confessor, portray God's creation of the human race as a risk willingly taken by the Creator, who thenceforward assumes an infinite vulnerability. The Fall – a symbol of such power that we experience it at every moment – becomes the proof of freedom, the proof without which we should not know that personal love exists. When God banished humankind from the Tree of Life, it was so that they should not go into eternity while in a state of separation. If they had been thrust just as they stood into the divine Light, that state (which we also share) could have been nothing other than hell, hell beyond recall. How often have we offended the steady gaze of an innocent child by our lying and depravity? The merest instant of love betrayed, of confidence ridiculed, if only we could see it with the perfect clarity of God's vision, would be revealed as an eternity in hell. How much we need the whole story from God, his patient instruction, the freedom that the cross of Christ can bring!

The condition of death brought about by sin is not a punishment, or is at the most a self-inflicted one which God turns into a cure. Death is the result of rejecting the living God, excluding the Creator from his creation. But God was to take flesh and die, in order to fill death itself with his love and turn it into resurrection for the human race.

From Pharisaism to the mystery of freedom

An anthropology which embraces such a notion of sin will deal with good and evil in terms not of moral value, but of being and non-being, life and death, communion and separation, disease and healing. And the Church addresses us in the same terms: we are to be grafted by baptism on to the living Body of the Risen Christ, and thus enabled to receive the power of the resurrection by which our life can be plucked from death, death in all its forms. So it is with Lazarus as we see him depicted in the icons: in response to the royal summons of the one who can say, '*I am* the resurrection and the life,' he bursts from the tomb; he is still bound with grave-clothes, but already they are falling away.

By the grace of the lifegiving cross, we receive power to trans-form every state of death into a state of resurrection. By baptism in Christ, in the Holy Spirit, in the Father's house the Church, we are restored to the likeness of God, sharing in the divine life as the image becomes clearer. Then we can experience the great bap-tismal initiation, dying and descending into hell with Christ in order to be born in him to a new life made fruitful by eternity. Then we can try to die to our own death, our non-existence, on which the loss of our freedom confers a paradoxical kind of existence. We die to sadistic love, to the master-slave relationship, to the despair concealed by pride, so that we can be reborn in the infinite space of the Body of Christ where the Spirit breathes, where we are 'members one of another', where every face is enlightened from within in an everlasting Pentecost.

Christian life entails, at its main stages, indeed at every moment, an 'Easter', a gradual metamorphosis of our whole being. In the light of the death-and-resurrection of baptism we understand significant moments in our lives – of parting, suffering, forsakenness when we 'descend into hell', fervour, intoxication, bedazzlement when we 'return to paradise' – as moments of ini-tiation. Passing from successive partial deaths to foreshadowed resurrections, we come at last to the final 'passover' of death which, since we have already left death behind us, becomes a peaceful 'dormition', the entrance into the more perfect light and life of the communion of saints.

For human beings today, so deeply influenced by the great reductionists of the 19th and early 20th centuries, this anthro-pology is a possible means to freedom.

Just as there are Fathers of the Church, there are also what we might call Fathers of the modern world, revered and studied by the intelligentsia, who hope to combine them in a sort of grand synopsis of atheism. We may never have read Feuerbach, Marx, Nietzche or Freud, but our outlook, the spirit of the age, is formed by their ideas.

The Marxist theory of social alienation and the reification of humanity the creator in the 'master-slave' dialectic, leaves us with a God who is nothing but the essence of human alienation (*nothing but* being the characteristic formula of reductionism). Nietzche's philosophy of the will for power, health, status, creative amusement, reduces God to the product of a 'platonism for the people', a world of illusions, a refuge for our weakness and a weapon to arm our resentment. Then there are the great advances in psychoanalysis. Freud's discovery of the super-ego, nourished by obsessive guilt, makes God the projection of the sadistic father. Jung demonstrated that a would-be Christian is often so only at the level of clear self-awareness; at this level we tend to identify evil and impurity with the dark, womblike and teeming depths of our own nature. Lucifer, however, was an angel of light!

Human understanding, acute but autonomous according to the great reductionists, must become for us an *ascetic understanding*. It must help us to see how the encumbrances of history, class-consciousness, resentment, the tragedy of sex and the awareness of death, are constantly tarnishing the image of God in us, and constantly raising up masks and idols which distort the mystery. Thus we shall progress, as even Nietzche sometimes desired, from the 'moral God' to the 'divine God'.

It is no accident that the great reductionists formulated their critique at a time when Christianity had degenerated into morality. And morality itself had degenerated into infantile repression by the super-ego, a castrating anxiety about purity, or its sublimation into a kind of angelism bordering on dissociation, almost to the point of schizophrenia, between the orderly ideal and intractable real life. At bottom, is it not true that the notion of salvation had become a matter of paying a price through suffering; that the sins (in the plural) with which we were obsessed were seen as breakings of rules; that our salvation through Christ's death on the cross, was seen as an exaction of divine vengeance, forgetting that the cross of death is also the cross of glory, that the Disfigured is also the Transfigured?

In their frantic search for liberty – or to be more accurate, licence – in every sphere of modern life, people think they are breaking free from the obsessive concerns of morality, the life-denying other-worldliness, the pharisaical preoccupation with purity, in order to recover a more spontaneous and innocent attitude to existence. They hope to recapture, in the face of what they regard as Christian taboos and hypocritical moral prohibitions, a 'Dionysiac' freedom, 'a world where there is no such thing as sin', as the publicity for the *Satyricon* said. They entertain the desperate hope that the Fall itself might be the way back to the innocence of paradise, the means by which the self can break free from its limitations. But if the self is not exposed, by a personal faith, to the absolute Source of life, it will be in danger of disintegration in the impersonal force of nature. The 'revolution' of popular mythology has been a welcome excuse. The self is torn between orgasmic frenzy on the one hand and nostalgic world-weariness on the other. There is a profound description of the latter state in the novel by Alberto Moravia called, simply, *L'Ennui*: 'My feeling of ennui springs from the absurd notion that reality is not enough; I realize that I cannot escape from myself, but also that I might escape if some unimaginable miracle were to happen.'

It seems to me that the Christian attitude towards this quest for freedom should be above all one of respect. In sin, especially when it is pursued through thick and thin, regardless of the consequences, the whole paradox of human nature is revealed. The divine image is obscured but clear enough to point to its Archetype. We need to be able to recognize the yearning for the infinite, for freedom and communion, the determination not to sink into an unthinking conventional spirituality, the suffering entailed in the search for the absolute in a world which can offer no salvation but is itself waiting to be saved. According to the young revolutionaries, to be grown up is to have given up the struggle, an acquiescence as adults which is adultery. They wish their adolescence could go on for ever because their only experience of the Spirit is their own youthful vitality, which is still running at full strength. They cannot put into words what they are looking for, they do not know its Name, but they feel the thirst. And within the adult, in whom madness is often evidence of freedom, we must discern the person still passionately and blindly yearning for fulfilment, since we know for certain that even in deepest hell, Christ, who has conquered hell for eternity, waits for the person called in the Book of Revelation 'the one who thirsts'.

Here we can cite two great witnesses. Denys the Aeropagite writes (*Divine Names* 4.20): 'The libertine is deprived of good by his irrational lust; we can say that the privation annihilates him in some way, also that his lust has no real object. Nevertheless, because there remains in him a faint echo of communion and friendship, he still shares in the Good. In the same way, anger shares in the Good by its intrinsic desire to bring about an improvement in something it sees as bad. Even one who desires the worst possible life, since it is a desire for life, and a life which seems the best, by the mere desire to live, by reaching out towards life, that person has some part in the Good.'

And St John Climacus (*Heavenly Ladder* 5.6.57): 'I have seen impure souls, who were possessed by carnal love to the point of fury and madness, at last embrace penitence and, thanks to their experience of physical *eros*, and its conversion into divine *eros*, become enflamed with love for the Creator, transcending all servile fear. That is why Jesus Christ did not say of the chaste sinner that she had feared much, but that she had loved much ...'

Thus the experience of separation and of desire, unavoidable for everyone destined to rise again, becomes the spiritual turning-point. While we are looking to the 'passions' for fulfilment, our desire for the infinite is doomed to be frustrated. Once we realize this, we discover that God alone can satisfy the need which is basic to our nature.

Origen has described a striking vision of the soul plumbing the depths of evil by experiencing the horror of excess; after actually dying, having journeyed through the infernal regions, it eventually realizes that evil has its limitations, that one can be surfeited with it to the point of utter boredom. Then God is revealed as alone inexhaustible, to whom everyone, even Satan, will turn in the end.

The Church has condemned the Origenist belief in the certainty of universal salvation, since that would make salvation automatic, indeed compulsory. But it has absorbed the hope which the teaching contains and expressed it in a highly spiritual form as a prayer of universal compassion that all might be saved.

Metanoia, the complete turning round in a person's heart of hearts, is not an attempt to achieve some superficial mental improvement by an effort of will, to overcome some fault or vice. It is first and foremost the utter trusting in Christ who gives himself up to death, hell and separation for us, for me; to the death which I have caused, to the hell which I create and in which I make others and myself live, to the separation which is my condition and my sin. By enduring them, he has made death, hell and torment the door of repentance and new life. Then we discover something we never dared hope for, that our hellish autonomy has been breached by sin, death, and despair, that these have opened us to the mercy of the living God. Then the heart of stone becomes a heart of flesh, the stone which sealed the fountain of life in our heart is shattered; then gush forth the tears of repentance and wonderment, washing us in the waters of baptism, the great waters sanctified by Christ in the beginning, in which we are purified and recreated by the Spirit.

Turning back

What is required of us above all is an entreaty, a cry of trust and love *de profondis*, from the depths of our heart. For a moment we must lose our balance, must see in a flash of clarity the meaninglessness of suffering, the ripping apart of our protective covering of happiness or moral virtue. Remember how often in the Gospels Christ attacks the Pharisees. Remember, in *Crime and Punishment*, the terror which seizes Sonia, the humble prostitute, when she reads the Gospel of the raising of Lazarus to Raskolnikov, the contemptible superman who discovers that he is after all only a murderer. Remember, in the same book, the monologue of the grotesque Marmeladov, Sonia's father, who by his baseness, cowardice and drunkenness has lost his family. He, the fallen, just before his death, gives this account of the Last Judgement: 'Then Christ will say to us, Come you also! Come you drunkards! Come you weaklings! Come you depraved! And he will say to us, Vile creatures, you are in the image of the beast and you bear his mark. All the same, you come too!

'And the wise and prudent will say, Lord, why are you welcoming them? And he will say, O wise and prudent, I am welcoming them because not one of them has ever judged himself worthy. And he will stretch out his arm to us, and we shall fall at his feet, and burst into sobs, and then we shall understand everything, everything! Lord, your kingdom come!'

As we begin the Christian life we need to discover our own finiteness, and at the same time our longing for the infinite, that we are not self-sufficient, that we have not the source of joy within ourselves, that at every moment we must receive ourselves at the Father's merciful hand – and this word 'Father' resounds with all the depth of the Unknowable and the wonderful trust of the child discovering his origin. In the Gospel the very root of sin is the pretence that we can save ourselves by our own effort, that we can find security in ourselves and one another. This was the condition the Pharisees had been brought to in the end by their strict keeping of the law. To save ourselves we must give up all security, any notion of being self-sufficient; we must look at the world with wonder, gratefully receiving it anew, with its mysterious promise of the infinite. Everything – the world, history, other people and myself – can be a source of revelation, because through everything we can discern, like a watermark, the face of the Risen Christ, the Friend who secretly shares with each of us the bread of affliction and the wine of mirth. To this paradox, that the Inaccessible has allowed himself to be crucified for us to reveal that 'God is love', our only response can be one of humility and trust, tearing ourselves away from all that holds us back, in our desire to worship, even in the midst of our suffering. The publicans and harlots enter the Kingdom before the just because they are well aware that they cannot save themselves; knowing the wretchedness of their condition, they are open to the Love that has come within their reach. So the turning back is not only the result of guilty feelings. It is the consciousness of a desire that cannot be satisfied, the inner emptiness crying out to be filled with it knows not what. 'The hearts of human beings,' says Nicolas Cabasilas, 'were made great enough to contain God himself' (*Life in Christ*, 2.E). If they do not contain the Uncreated they will turn their desire towards created objects, and then only nothingness can spring forth, for every person is a gaping space waiting to be filled with God.

Repentance entails consciously becoming 'the one who thirsts', and at the same time recognizing the wretched nature of the idols with which we try to deceive this desire; the wretched nature of 'this world', the net of passions in which we think to catch creation while forgetting the Creator; the wretchedness of our own role, or roles, in the great theatre of 'this world'.

Then we discover the basic truth about ourselves, that we are loved, and it is because we are loved that we exist.

And love responds to love. The awareness of being loved and the response that it unlocks are the only criterion of repentance.

'The scribes and the Pharisees brought a woman who had been caught in adultery, and placing her in the midst they said to him, "Master, this woman has been caught in adultery, in the very act.

Now in the law Moses commanded us to stone such. What do you say about her?"... But Jesus bent down and wrote with his finger on the ground. And as they continued to ask him, he stood up and said to them, "Let him who is without sin among you be the first to throw a stone at her!" And once more he bent down and wrote with his finger on the ground. But when they heard it, they went away, one by one, beginning with the eldest, and Jesus was left alone with the woman standing before him. Jesus looked up and said to her, "Woman, where are they? Has no one condemned you?" She said, "No one, Lord." And Jesus said, "Neither do I condemn you; go, and sin no more"' (John 8.3-11). An intolerable text! It is missing from several manuscripts. Our moral conscience, indeed our religious conscience, cannot admit that Christ refuses to condemn this woman who says nothing, who shows no repentance. She has been taken *in delicto flagrante*; the crime she has committed is one of the most serious known to the Law, not only because it undermines the patriarchal structure of Jewish society, but because Scripture describes the relationship of God with his chosen people in terms of marital faithfulness and unfaithfulness. Christ confounds her accusers by reminding them that evil is universal: spiritually, they also are adulterers; they also, in one way or another, have betrayed love. 'Let him who is without sin ...' No one is without sin. And he concludes by saying, 'Go and sin no more', giving her a new start in life.

Being aware of our state of separation, while longing to end it, is a prerequisite of the breaking up of the superficial self, of the shattering of our stony heart. Without this breaking up, Christ cannot be resurrected in me. That is why the monks say that repentance is the 'reminder of death', making us personally aware of our state of separation.

St John Climacus says, 'To define repentance as the awareness of individual guilt is to risk emptying it of meaning' (*Sermons*, ed. Constantinople, p.118). Again, to define sin as mere individual guilt would be to do without God, since all we should have to do in order to quieten our conscience would be to keep the Law. But, as St Paul reminds us, the law cannot 'make alive' (Galatians 3.21). We who are reminded every day of our death, that is of the daily murder of love, know that only the victory of Christ over hell and death can 'make alive'.

Once we have made this great return journey across the flood, receiving presentiments of the nature of death, we are thenceforward filled with a sorrowful joy. Our whole being is pervaded by a tenderness which is not the denial of passion, but its transfiguration by the passion of the Lord. We become capable of receiving others no longer as enemies but as brothers and sisters – this is the mysterious 'love of enemies' of the Gospel – of welcoming them without judging them, and perhaps of finding the right words to enlighten them in their turn. Without any effort on our part, we become different in our most ordinary words and actions, and may succeed in conveying to others that there is a meaning to life, that death has not the last word.

The outlook of a person who is in Christ cannot be understood except through penitence and prayer. Even then, if we speak of it at all, we shall preserve a certain reticence out of respect for the promise of life, the possibility of beauty, which we have learnt to discern in the individual person, as in the history of the human race. The words which spring from a purified heart can take root in the heart of another. In the same way Moses, on Sinai, could see God only 'from behind', and in the same way words become, so to speak, the other side of silence, the other side of peace. And this peace, from the resurrection appearances to the disciples – 'Peace be with you' – down to the liturgical celebrations of today – 'In peace let us pray to the Lord' – testifies to the presence of the Risen Christ. The gentleness of strong people makes them trees of peace – 'he is like a tree planted by the waterside... and his leaf shall not wither' (Psalm 1.3-4). We have massacred the trees under the illusion that they are useful for nothing. And now we realise that without trees the earth is no longer fruitful. This age needs people like trees, filled with a silent peace, rooted at the same time in solid ground and in the open sky.

2

The Person in the Image of God

The human being as creature

We are created, we are creatures; this basic statement of faith sums up the truth that we are not self-sufficient, that we cannot find fulfilment without turning towards the unknown God who holds us in existence and calls us to himself.

We must avoid static, objectifying language, as if the Creator and his creature existed side by side. Creatures exist only in God, in that creative will which is precisely what distinguishes him from his creation. We must all, one day, utter in our own words the excellent prayer of Dostoevsky's wanderer, Makar: 'Everything is in thee, my God; I myself am in thee; receive me.' God will always welcome us, but only if we freely ask to be received.

'Creatures,' wrote Metropolitan Philaret of Moscow in the last century, 'are balanced upon the creative will of God as upon a bridge of diamond; above is the abyss of the divine infiniteness and below is the abyss of their own nothingness.' Nothingness, by definition, is not 'something'. It is a limiting concept signifying that the human being does not exist by itself but that God is 'its beginning, its middle and its end' (St Maximus the Confessor), that it is in God, as Paul told the Athenians, 'that we live and move and have our being' (Acts 17.28).

So we cannot exist apart from God or outside of God. No one can. By the very life in us we are rooted in the one living God. In Islam there is a saying that the first cry of the newborn and the last sigh of the dying together compose and utter the divine Name.

Each heartbeat is an act of faith. Living cannot but be celebration. That is why Alyosha Karamazov tries to dissuade his brother Ivan from nihilism, begging him to love life, to dare to abandon himself to the great love that is within him; only afterwards will it make sense to him. And it is why even today, despite the apparent victory of nihilism, there are so few suicides.

Through loving life we become aware that God's grace is prevenient, that existence apart from him is impossible, because life is inseparable from grace.

'Then the Lord God formed man of dust from the ground, and breathed into his nostrils the breath of life; and man became a living being' (Genesis 2.7).

The Fathers are constantly commenting on this passage, saying that uncreated grace, which is light and fire, is implicit in the act of creation itself. Humanity receives life and grace at the same time. From the beginning grace is inherent in the very fact of existing.

Gregory of Nazianzus even speaks of an 'outpouring of divinity' (*On the Soul* PG.XXVII.452). For him, the life within us is the actual breath of God, the Holy Spirit, who not only broods over the waters at creation, but is concentrated in the life of the human person, where the universal life is completed and transcended.

In countries where Orthodoxy has been influential, literature, even when avowedly atheist, bears witness to this essential grace. In their own way the novels of Kazakov or the songs of Theodorakis express gratitude for the gift of life. The same gratitude transforms the 'tragic nihilism' of Kazantzakis. Wherever Eastern Christianity has left its mark there remains an awareness of divine forces, even when God is denied.

The human vocation is to become the willing and conscious celebrant of this great mystery. The only truly natural person is the one who is aware of being a creature drawn by grace, called to union with the Creator.

There is no middle ground. Modern humanism was able to spread only because it had been secretly carried within the

Christian revelation of the divine-human. The death of God brings about the death of Man. Gregory of Nyssa used to say that if a person's face is not clothed in the light of the Spirit it will wear the mask of a demon; and the danger is that the mask will take flesh, turn into a snout. In our own time Nicholas Berdyaev has said that the meaning of history eventually resolves itself into the choice between the divine-human and the bestial-human.

The origin of the the idea of the person: trinitarian theology

As creatures we possess not only a created nature but personal identity.

We think we know instantly what a person is. To judge from what philosophers and psychologists say, you would think that whatever is best in the individual determines what the person is. Whereas the theologian knows that the person is a mystery, intelligible only by the contemplation of the Trinity.

The priestly prayer of Christ in St John's Gospel puts it in a nutshell: 'That they may all be one; even as thou, father, art in me, and I in thee, that they also may be in us... The glory which thou hast given me I have given to them, that they may be one even as we are one, I in them and thou in me ...' (John 17.21-22).

However, it was not until the 4th century that the theology of the Trinity was fully developed, in response to two explanations which tended to contradict each other; one that confused the divine Persons, the other that separated them. Between the first Ecumenical Council at Nicaea and the second at Constantinople, St Athanasius emphasized the mystery of the essential oneness of the Son and of the Father. In relation to the Father, the Son is *homoousios*; that is to say, not of the 'same' substance – 'same' might indicate a mere likeness – but absolutely *identical* in being.

A little later the Cappadocians – Basil of Caesarea, Gregory of Nazianzus, Gregory of Nyssa – emphasized, in an antinomic argument, the irreducible difference between the Father and the Son:

the Son is identical in substance with the Father, but he is at the same time absolutely unique, as also the Father is unique. And it was the Cappadocians who showed that the Holy Spirit, who for long had been confused with the divine presence which he communicates to us, also shares in that 'consubstantiality', while remaining absolutely and mysteriously unique.

In their desire to do justice to the glory of the living God, the Fathers of the 4th century precipitated a revolution of language and thought.

The great biblical revelation of *I* and *thou*, the self and the other, was a difficult notion for ancient philosophy. Sometimes, in the 'initiatory' tradition developed by Plotinus, whereby beings return by a process of conversion to their origin, *thou* and *I* were obliterated in the impersonal One; sometimes individuals were represented as similar but separate. Traces of this uncertainty can be seen in the vocabulary. The Greek *prosopon* and the Latin *persona* alike retain something of their original meaning, which is a theatrical mask. That is why the Fathers left these words to one side, preferring to use a common term but with a new meaning. They took one not from philosophy but from everyday life, where it served to designate a thing, as distinct from other things: *hypostasis*. We shall translate it as Person, with a capital, to avoid any confusion with philosophical usage.

'Hypostasis' was almost a synonym for *ousia*, a component of *homoousios*, meaning substance, nature – quite simply, a thing. However, as we have said, the first of these words emphasised distinctness, the second what is shared. The Fathers used 'hypostasis' of the Father, the Son or the Holy Spirit, each in its incomparable originality. And they called their identity *ousia*.

By this antinomy they defined the very mystery of Love.

Fallen logic opposes or confuses. The dogma of the Trinity suggests the coincidence, in the divine Source, of absolute unity and absolute diversity. Three, here, is a 'meta- mathematical' number (St Basil of Caesarea) which, always identical to the One, signifies the infinite transcending of opposition, not by reabsorption in the impersonal, but in the fulness of love, whereby each Person, in his transparent difference, far from vying with the others, gives importance to them. Each is uniquely the means of giving existence to the same Substance, of receiving it from the others and of imparting it to them in what Maximus the Confessor calls the 'motionless movement of love', a loving dance in which each effaces himself to give fuller existence to the others, and thereby is fully himself.

So the Trinity, the *Identity of Unique Persons*, signifies that love is not merely the fulfilment of personal existence but its origin.

Person and nature

First I shall describe the mystery of the created Person in its vertical relation, on the one hand to God who calls it, and on the other to the human nature which it must assume, and whose 'panhuman' and cosmic aspects we shall study in the following chapters.

Vladimir Lossky has shown clearly that the supernatural character of the person runs right through the Chalcedonian definition. This emphasizes the unity of the humanity and the divinity. Christ is true God and true man, he is perfect in his humanity. This humanity in its wholeness embraces the visible and the invisible, the body and the 'reasonable' soul. 'Reasonable' is a poor translation of the Greek, which means the spirit, the fine point of the soul, the spiritual capacity by which human nature is opened to the Spirit. Christ's humanity is therefore complete, comprising a spiritual soul and a body. However, he is not a human person, since he is the incarnate Word, the Son co-eternal with the Father, and therefore a divine Person. In other words, in the human being the person is not identifiable with the body, or the soul, or the spirit. It arises from another order of reality.

We can see that in Christian anthropology the fundamental distinction is not between the body and the soul, or between the body and the spirit. The Fathers and the ascetics, despite the influence of Hellenic dualism, have stayed faithful to the biblical understanding of the human being as a unity which God radically transcends and which he can entirely transfigure. So a truly Christian approach has no difficulty with the psychosomatic unity on which modern human science lays such emphasis.

The real distinction is between the *nature* and the *person*.

When we ask of something, 'What is *it*?' we are seeking to learn about its nature. The question, being an abstract idea, is neutral. The person, however, goes beyond all questions. It cannot be defined, it cannot be captured by conceptual thought.

The person, says Lossky, is 'the irreducibility of the individual to his human nature', the person is irreducible. In the non-Christian East reduction is by ascetic practice, in the post-Christian West by science. The Eastern method removes the dead layers, cosmic, biological, social, psychological, and reabsorbs the human being in the transpersonal. The Western method concentrates on the health of the infrapersonal, analysing its conditionings and curing them by psychoanalysis or social revolution.

But what the person desires is deified humanity. It acts in collusion with the living God, being like him secret, mysterious, incomprehensible. Deep calls to deep. The only approach to the mystery of the living God is by means of 'negative' theology, which denies all possibility of limiting God to the capacity of our thoughts. And the only approach to the created person is through a 'negative' anthropology. Here the ascetic practices of the non-Christian East and the scientific analyses of the West are most valuable, not because they tell us what the person is, but because they help us to understand what it is not. To know something of the mystery of the person, we must go right beyond its natural context, beyond its cosmic, collective, and individual environment, beyond all the ways in which it can be grasped by the mind. Whatever the mind can grasp can only be the nature, never the person. The mind can grasp only objects, whatever is open to inspection. But the person is not an object open to inspection, any more than God is. Like God it is incomparable, inextinguishable, fathomless.

Individuals can be classified or grouped. But the person is always unique. It breaks groups apart, it is itself a breach in the universe.

To begin to discern the mystery of the person, we must push further the parallel between negative theology and negative anthropology. God is 'greater than God', beyond all affirmation, even beyond all negation. The Depth is revealed as the Lover who transcends his own transcendence and comes to seek for the 'lost sheep' – the whole of humanity and every single one of us – and to become for us the 'bread of life'. The true name of the living God is the one he took for himself when on the cross he revealed himself as Love. Negative theology leads us to the paradox of the crucified God, the unapproachable God who while giving himself totally yet remains veiled by the very brilliance of his light. The more we find God, and the more we seek him, the more deeply we are brought into the inexhaustible mutual exchange of the One in Three.

And as, through Christ, this life of the Trinity is shed abroad, we find the same thing happening in the way we know our neighbour. The person, set by its very brilliance beyond the reach of rational analysis, is revealed in love. This disclosure surpasses all other ways of knowing a human being; it requires prayer, attentiveness, even to the point of dying to oneself; knowing a person is *unknowing*, the darkness of night made luminous by love.

Then, momentarily at first, we see the open face, that place where nature most readily allows the person to show through, first by the transparency of the eyes. For a moment, the face is seen, not weighed down by nature, but in God. Then we see everything from the opposite side. The person, far from deriving its meaning from the world in which it is immersed, suddenly illuminates the world by its presence and interprets it to us. The frets of time and pain on our flesh, the weariness which drags it down, the wrinkles which wither it, all become a miraculous sign of a personal existence. Our capacity for astonishment is renewed and refreshed.

'The tree was almost covered in snow; its twigs and berries were half iced over. Two snow-laden boughs reaching out to him in welcome reminded him of Lara's long white arms, their beautiful generous curve. He clung to them, pulling the tree towards him. As if in answer the rowan tree let fall a shower of snow which covered him from head to foot. Not knowing what he said, he muttered, "I'll find you, my beauty, my princess, my rowan tree, my treasure, my love"' (Boris Pasternak. *Doctor Zhivago* Ch.12).

It is always tempting to judge rather than to accept. We are always labelling other people. If we are labelling them we are no longer seeing them. By knowledge, especially knowledge of other people, we achieve self-assurance, or the justification of our desires. Every form of sadism has been justified by collective hatred. The torturer and the perverted lover have this in common, that they wish to possess a person. But one can only possess corpses. True knowledge of some one else, that is unknowing, demands at the same time risk and respect. God has not truly known the human race except on the cross. *An infinite vulnerability is the condition of this unknowing, where the more the known is known, the more it is revealed as unknown.*

No, the God of Christians is not the summit – reassuring and plain to see – of a pyramid of beings. He is the depth who reveals depths everywhere, making of the most familiar creature a thing unknown. We are like drunken potholers; every face we see reveals the hidden side of the earth.

It is a wonderful and compelling vision.

'Do not try to distinguish between the worthy and the unworthy; all must be equal in your eyes to love and to serve ... Did not the Lord share the table of publicans and harlots, without putting away the unworthy from him? Thus you shall confer the same benefits, the same honours ... on the faithless and the murderer, forasmuch as he is also your brother, since he shares in the same human nature' (St Isaac of Syria, sentence 11).

The vocation of St Thérèse of Lisieux was born of her prayer for a murderer whose terrible fate was reported in the newspapers. She felt like his mother.

Murderers are the sort of people whom we would rather ignore. But the first to whom Christ gave the assurance, 'this day you shall be with me in paradise', was a murderer on the gallows. It was there that the mystery of the person was consecrated.

In the 20th century, philosophical reductionism has become historical reductionism. Who can tell the connection between Nietzsche and Hitler, between Marx and Stalin, between Pavlov and Freud and the society of emptiness and 'happiness'? The blood of the martyrs, and above all their prayer for their tormentors, witnessed in the Soviet Union as well as in the Nazi camps, testifies to the irreducible character of the person.

So many rebellions of today – pursued with a vigour out of all proportion to their original causes – are evidence that we desire transcendence and joy, and not this happiness with which people are obsessed, which is the happiness of livestock, well nourished, well washed, well psychoanalysed, force-fed with agreeable sensations and scientifically achieved orgasms. If we had recipes for ecstasy we should even be free from the need for repentance. But the human being is a person in the image of God and the image aspires towards its Pattern.

Humanity in God's image

The ancient philosophers loved to stress the central place of Man in the universe. They said that Man is the only animal which stands upright, and so symbolizes the dimensions of space, first the high, or heavenly, and the low, or earthly. Other animals walk on all fours or crawl. Their space is purely earthly; it is only by Man that they are connected to the heavens. True, trees and rocks stand upright, symbolizing the world's vertical axis, but they cannot move; they are not free to choose a right or wrong direction, to express or repress the prayer which is, however blindly, their essential nature, their mysterious 'sacramentality'.

This symbolism is familiar to all the great spiritual traditions. In the Far East, for example, Man is portrayed in an ideogram as the intermediary between earth and heaven. And the Japanese, when arranging flowers, place a horizontal branch for the earth, a vertical one for heaven, and a third in the middle, to represent Man the cosmic mediator.

The Fathers developed this theme, emphasizing that human beings unite in themselves the visible and the invisible, and thus sum up the universe. But for the Fathers humanity's true glory is never the summing up of the universe, but always its being made in the image of God. 'There is nothing remarkable,' writes Gregory of Nyssa, 'in Man's being the image and likeness of the universe, for earth passes away and the heavens change... in thinking we exalt human nature by this grandiose name (microcosm, synthesis of the universe) we forget that we are thus favouring it with the qualities of gnats and mice' (PG.XLIV.1770-1801).

The friend of Gregory of Nyssa, Gregory of Nazianzus, said, 'In my earthy character, I am attached to the life I have down here, but being also a divine particle, I bear in my heart the desire for immortality' (PG.XXXVII.452).

So human beings, like God, are personal beings. Human nature is not blind, like that of a rock or a tree. A human being must consciously and responsibly embody, express and explain his or her nature; by means of it he or she must answer the call of God. The image is therefore not *something* within humanity; it is at once the fulfilment a human being's nature longs for and the basis of personal freedom.

In many ancient traditions, as still today in India, salvation is understood as dissolution into the vastness of the universe, reabsorption into an impersonal divinity; but the Fathers insist that humanity must 'personalize' the universe; not save itself by means of the universe, but save it by communicating grace to it. And all the while human beings must also humbly decipher the 'Bible of the world'; they elevate themselves above all life in order to bring it to fruition, giving voice to and encouraging its secret surge of praise. The modern will to dominate nature as if it were something mechanical, an assemblage of things and forces which we use without respect, is just as foreign to true Christianity as it is to the impersonal cosmization of the East. Might not the loveless power of the West today be the obverse of a Christianity which has become an individualistic religion of the 'soul' – 'God and my soul' – unable to assume the depths of the nature within and around humankind?

In an Eastern garden or engraving, nature is dissolved subtly in waters and mists, in which a faceless eternity is condensed and hidden. In a Western megalopolis, nature is devoured by technology; the human race, in its power and its pleasures, reigns supreme; God's heaven, the vastness of the sky, is riddled with noise, obscured by fog; God's night, of suffering and of faith, is abolished by lights.

A Romanesque or Byzantine church is at the same time an expression of the earth and a benediction; surrounding nature has been humanised by the patient love of humankind, the blood of the martyrs, the tombs signed with the cross of victory; this mastery does not obliterate, but releases prayer from things. In the silence of the crypt, holy water and the Black Virgin intensify the womb-like holiness of the earth. In the apse or in the dome, benediction shines from heaven in a face – the human face of God, the Icon of the risen Lord.

Then the question arises: Why has God created us tragically free, tragically responsible – so heavy a burden that we constantly lay it down at the feet of idols and inquisitors? To which the great Christian Tradition replies unanimously: God created us free because he summons us to deification – to a divine-human condition in which our transformed humanity will find its fulfilment. This call demands a free response. Union that resulted from mere magnetic force would be automatic, instinctive, unworthy of a personal existence which, even in its wish for union, requires complete responsibility.

There does exist, it is true, an impersonal love which is the working of desire. Some contemplatives have stressed the spontaneous return of nature towards its origin. Denys the Areopagite, for example, saw the world as a kind of immense liturgy, a sacred dance revolving round the divine Centre, held in its attractive force. However, Denys was accepted into the Tradition only when corrected by Maximus the Confessor who, in his own writings and experience, emphasized the terrible freedom of Man.

That is why Adam had to undergo the test of freedom, to grow in maturity towards a conscious love. That is why sacrificial Love could not be revealed until Abraham's knife had glinted in the eyes of Isaac or until Job's cry had resounded, calling on God to transcend his own power. That is why the chosen people were a stiff-necked people, who got their name – Israel – after wrestling in the dark with the unnamed Stranger. That is why, finally, when God took on himself the destiny of Isaac and of Job, he came in secret, so that only by the free love of humankind could he be recognized in a crucified slave, defiled with blood and spittle. Even the risen Lord does not force himself on our presence; it was with a cry of faith and love that Mary Magdalen recognized him in the garden, and the beloved disciple on the lake shore. Our God comes in secret, and the Church herself, where we are united by the Spirit to the eucharistic body of the risen Christ, is a secret whose holiness is hidden from us by all the detritus of history. We can really love God only because we can refuse him. The book in the Bible which most clearly expresses this truth is possibly the Song of Songs, where the one painstakingly seeks the other. God seeks us more than we seek God.

God's risk

The human being, the being who is personal, is the pinnacle of creation. With humanity the omnipotence of God gives rise to something radically new. Not a lifeless reflection or a puppet, but a freedom which can oppose God, and put the fulfilment of God's creation in jeopardy by excluding him from it. In the supreme achievement of God's creative omnipotence – for only lifegiving Love can create a free living being – there is an inherent risk. Omnipotence finds fulfilment in self-limitation. In the creative act itself, God in some manner limits himself, withdraws, to give human beings space in which to be free. At its highest point omnipotence thus conceals a paradoxical impotence; because the summit of omnipotence is love, and God can do everything except force human beings to love. To enter into love, as we know, is to put ourselves without protection at the mercy of the worst suffering, that of rejection and abandonment by the one we love. Creation is in the shadow of the cross. The Lamb of God, according to the Book of Revelation, is slain from the foundation of the world.

The divine will always lays itself open to the trials and errors, the waywardness, the rebelliousness of humanity, in order to lead it, perhaps, to a free consent. Thus does the Lord train us. By itself this might seem a weak image if we think of God as the beggar of love waiting at the gate of the soul and never daring to force it. 'In fact, he is not content with calling to him the slave whom he has loved, but he comes down and looks for him himself; he the rich, draws near to our poverty, he offers himself, declares his love and begs us to return it; in the face of rejection, he does not go away, he takes no offence at injury; if repulsed, he waits at the door and does everything to show himself a true lover; he suffers wounds and dies ... ' (Nicholas Cabasilas, *Life in Christ*, VI.A.I).

The love of God is thus the space in which I am free. If God is not, I am no more than a particle of society and of the universe, subject to their determinisms, eventually to death. But if God is crucified Love, I am offered freedom without bounds, a share of the freedom of God himself.

Maximus the Confessor clearly distinguishes two freedoms in Man: that of his nature and that of his person. The first is the magnetic attraction of his deepest being towards God, the completion of his nature in love; indeed, Man desires love with his whole nature and finds fulfilment in it. Human beings conceal within themselves an 'immense capacity for love and joy which is effective from the moment it knows the presence of the Beauty par excellence, the Beloved' (Nicholas Cabasilas, *ibid*. II.E). In the great union of love, human nature finds what it desires, the attainment of spontaneity, of freedom.

It is Christ who brings about this restoration of fullness. We have only to be grafted, by baptism and the eucharist, on to his deifying body, for this unifying energy to spring up from our inner depths.

But Maximus reminds us that there is another, strictly personal freedom, which cannot be constrained, or modified in any way from outside.

Although Christ restores and renews our nature, he cannot take upon himself our personal freedom, for the person is an absolute that nothing, not even God, can assume or transform. That freedom God can only appeal to by the example of his love. So he takes flesh, suffers and dies for us, for 'greater love has no man than this, that a man lay down his life for his friends'. By his love for human beings he is utterly destroyed; he allows the despair of separated humanity to enter into himself, to the point that an unthinkable chasm is opened between God and God, between the Father and the crucified Son, as if God dying in the flesh on the cross experienced atheism in its most hellish form: 'My God, my God, why hast thou forsaken me?' The infinite contradiction between the Living and the Crucified God is witness to humanity that God is infinite love, the love that Maximus the Confessor and Nicholas Cabasilas have called 'mad'.

'Two things in particular denote the lover and ensure his conquest: to do well to the beloved by every possible means, and if necessary to suffer evils and terrible torments on the beloved's behalf. The second proof is far superior to the first, but God, being impassible, was powerless to give it ... So he devised this 'humiliation', adapting himself in whatever way was necessary for him to be able to undergo evils and torments, so that those for whom he suffered might be convinced of his love' (Nicholas Cabasilas, *ibid*. VI.A.I).

So love responds to love, and personal freedom reawakens of its own accord. Eventually 'man surrenders only under the extreme pressure of God's humiliation' (Maximus the Confessor, *Second Letter to Thomas*).

In Christ, God loved his enemies more than himself. Such is the mystery of personal love. In the image of God, human beings become capable of loving others more than themselves – not more than their personal existence ('thou shalt love thy neighbour as thyself') but more than their own nature, their own life. Human beings become fully persons when they transcend their own nature in giving their life not only for their friends but for their enemies. That is why, according to the staretz Silhouan of Athos, the love of enemies is the only infallible criterion of our spiritual progress.

From image to likeness

Since we are in the image of God we are therefore in the image of Christ, and it is only in Christ that we discover the truth about ourselves. He alone is the one to whom the Beatitudes fully apply; the poor man who receives himself unceasingly at the hands of the Father and whose royal gentleness transforms the earth into a eucharist, the 'pure heart' like a still lake in which each discerns his true face; the witness of justice towards God and the brother against all the conformisms of power and pride; the crucified peacemaker who gives his life for his friends and restores his enemies to life. It is in the risen Lord that we discover the meaning of the world, the purpose of creation. The face of Christ is inseparably the face of God in man, the only face which is never closed because it is infinitely transparent, the only gaze which never petrifies but sets free. The face of faces, the key to all faces.

Everything was created by the Word with a view to his deifying incarnation. The Apostle says, 'In him all things were created, in heaven and on earth... all things were created through him and for him' (Col.1.16). In Christ the 'mystery hidden for ages and generations' (Col.1.26) is revealed, on which St Maximus comments, 'It was to this end, that is, the union in Christ of divinity and humanity, that God made all beings' (PG.XC.621 A). And Palamas is specific: 'Of humanity, created in his own image, God made Christ, so that humanity could not be separated from his pattern' (7th Homily for the feast of Lights).

At the very heart of the Trinity, we see the Son as humankind's eternal archetype, the heavenly man of whom the Old Testament prophets spoke, seeing in him the Pattern of humanity, the definitive Adam. For 'God has created human nature for no other purpose than to receive from it the mother whom he needed in order to be born' (Nicholas Cabasilas, *Marian Homily*). God's creation of the human race is to be seen from this divine-human perspective. The whole destiny of humanity is christological.

Incorporated in Christ by baptism we become again the image of God. But it is up to each of us to turn this image into the full likeness as we work out, under the breath and the fire of the Spirit, a personal, and therefore unique, way of being in Christ. 'God became the bearer of flesh so that humanity could become the bearer of the Spirit,' says Athanasius of Alexandria (PG.XXVI.996). Our freedom vies with the Spirit in love until finally they are united. Only then shall we be able to perfect the image and become the likeness, to give o*ur own face also* to the body of Christ. Little by little the Spirit and freedom are together assembling a mighty communion of all the transfigured, through which the universal transfiguration, already secretly realized in Christ, will manifest itself in glory. In Christ God opened to humanity the new and living way. Now he awaits humanity's free response, the 'newness of the Spirit' of which the Apostle speaks and which is present wherever persons live freely and creatively in communion. In the prayer and active love of those who 'breathe the Spirit' we see already springing up in anticipation the final victory over death, the final transformation of history and the universe which will be accomplished in the Kingdom.

'See how the Lord has given us the power to become eternally the children of God; henceforth our salvation is in our will' (Maximus the Confessor, PG.XC.953 B).

In the Mother of God, the first created person who has entered the resplendence of the Kingdom in her earthly flesh, we see the two mysteries conjoined: that of the image restored in Christ and that of the likeness achieved by the Spirit and freedom. Nicholas Cabasilas said that God, as long as he had not found a mother, was like a king in exile, like a stranger without a city. Solely because a young girl, in her sovereign freedom, received the angel's message, could God take flesh, re-enter the heart of his creation, recreate the world from within. For the body is simply the world as interior to a person, and only a person could readmit the Exile to the world through her body. There it was that the new Eve, for the first time since the original banishment, undid the tragedy of human freedom.

Today the mystery of Mary has become universal in the Church of the Holy Spirit. 'Christ is mysteriously born in the soul, taking flesh through those who are saved, making a virgin mother of the soul that gives birth to him' (Maximus the Confessor. PG,XC,889 C). The incarnation is not extended, but made actual in each person through the operation of the Holy Spirit. It is Christ who comes, the human Christ and the universal Christ, who is thus manifested little by little; he is identical with the risen Christ, but the Vine now bears innumerable clusters whence flows the wine of great joy. The Christ who comes will be in a new sense the Son of Man; every time the image of Christ, our pattern, bears fruit in a personal likeness according to the eternal youth of the Spirit, we bring him to birth.

A young Greek theologian, Panaghiotis Nellas, has observed that in the course of centuries many atheists have asserted that humanity could become God; but none of them, he says, has dared to think that human beings might give birth to God. That is what we affirm when we venerate the Mother of God, when we see in the faces of the saints the glorious advent of the Lord.

3

Persons in Communion

Singular and plural

Personal existence has a 'vertical' dimension, a desire to be plunged into the fullness of God. And this fullness is not a solitude but an ocean already alive with the movement of infinite love. The depth is not unrelieved gloom; it contains reciprocal activity, interchange, the presence of the other, while duality is avoided in the communion of the Three in One. The depth itself suggests the inexhaustible character of the Persons and of their love. We can now say boldly, 'God is love', without fear of blaspheming by appearing to trivialize. And if God is love, the person immersed in him is caught up in this movement, and opened to communion with his or her neighbour.

Throughout the Bible, singular and plural are treated as complementary. In the first chapter of Genesis we read, 'So God created man in his own image,... male and female he created them' (Genesis 1.27). This text is of course about man and woman, the polarization of nature, but it is just as relevant to the matter of singular and plural. My wife is before anything else my neighbour, even when I am tempted to forget it.

The mystery of the singular and the plural in humanity mirrors the mystery of the singular and the plural in God. Just as the essential unity of God is realized in personal love, so we are called to resemble God in realizing our essential unity with all humanity. Human nature, not the philosophical idea but the revealed truth,

cannot belong to a solitary being. It is distributed among persons
in all their variety; it resides in the great interchange of life by
which each exists for and through all the others. Christian spirituality – life in the Holy Spirit – is of its very nature something that
'we' share, our self-awareness being awakened by our sense of
being in communion with others. Never forget that this 'we' is not
an undifferentiated mass, that it has nothing to do with collective
hysteria. It exists always by personal encounter; it is my neighbour's face, innumerable certainly, but every time a face. The
Christian 'we' reflects the Trinity; in the Eastern liturgies, at the
threshold of the eucharistic mystery, the deacon proclaims, 'Let us
love one another, that with one mind we may confess ...', and the
choir replies, 'Father, Son and Holy Spirit, consubstantial, undivided Trinity.' The ancient kiss of peace which follows reminds us
that the Christian 'we', like the Trinity, is not a fusion, but a *unity
of unique persons.*

This is what distinguishes Christian spirituality from the mys-
ticisms and the metaphysics of the Self. Take, for example, the
state of 'enstasy', meaning reabsorption in the *Self*, not reaching
out towards Another. In India the word for it is *kaivalya*, 'forsakenness'. Huxley, Michaux, Junger and others, in their memorable
accounts of the use of drugs, describe the state of euphoria thus
attained as one of utter solitude, even when several people are
enjoying it together in the same place. At such a moment, the
presence of any stranger who was not having a parallel, similar,
experience of happiness, would cause intolerable distress. This
could never happen in genuine Christian life which, in the words
of Gregory of Nyssa, is an 'imitation of the Trinity'. Just as there is
one God in three Persons, so, in Christ, we are all 'members one of
another'; there is, and we are called to become, *a single Man in a
multitude of persons.*

The idea of a truly *trinitarian anthropology* is chiefly associated
with St Gregory of Nyssa, the most speculative of the
Cappadocians. In little tracts dismissed rather hastily by his

detractors as works of philology he attacks the 'erroneous custom' whereby Man is spoken of in the plural and God in the singular; in both cases personal plurality is quite consistent with unity of essence. We ought to say that in Christ, the new Adam, 'Man is unique in all men' (*There are not three Gods*, P.G., XLV, 117). 20th century Russian theology has returned to this assertion and refined it, as if to uncover the spiritual imperative, secularized though it may be, that socialism contains. Fr Sergius Bulgakov emphasized 'the total humanity of every person'. Fr Paul Florensky, who because of his sheer scholarship was allowed to stay in the Soviet Union, remarked that the fundamental difference between a truly Christian view of society and one based on the best intentioned social morality, is that while, according to the latter, people are merely alike, for the former they are in some sense 'consubstantial' like the Persons of the Trinity.

When we become living beings, we expand far beyond the limits of our own individuality into the vastness of the Body of Christ, no longer separated in space or time from any other being. Henceforth we carry within ourselves the whole of humanity.

In the light of these principles, history aquires its true significance. If there is only one human being, then all history is mine, since I am part of an immense communion. If history were only ruins and ashes, the history of death and the dead, why should we find it interesting? I am reminded of an incident in my childhood, when I was eight or nine years old. The entire world in which I was growing up, including school, was atheistic; it was not so much that God's existence was denied as that he was radically absent. One day in history, a subject I loved, the master was teaching us about the Emperor Charlemagne, crowned in the year 800, dead in 814. Dead... I suddenly felt dizzy. Dead, I said to myself, all the people in this book are dead. So why should I be interested in history? It was a long time before I found the answer: that history, in the end, is the destiny of humanity with God, and that our God is the God not of the dead but of the living.

The justification of the good

But sin turns this diverse unity into a hostile multiplicity, so that space becomes a separator, time a murderer, and language good only for expressing juxtaposition or possession. Whence the slogan of May 1968, 'Love one another'; this is facile blasphemy, because the erotic encounter itself is given us as a symbol, a foretaste of personal communion.

In the universe of sin solitary individuals devour one another. There is a besetting tendency today, when faced with a strictly spiritual predicament, where only holiness could work a cure, to explain it in terms that are purely historical, and ultimately socio-logical. So we speak of a consumer society, whereas, ever since the Fall, individuals have consumed one another incessantly, and together have consumed nature, which always retaliates with equal force. It is true that money is a powerful magnet that draws sin to the surface of the world, but it did not invent it:

> *The panting lover leans on his girl friend*
> *With the air of a dying man caressing his tomb,*

and the mother is tempted to devour her child rather than bring it truly into the world.

The universe of sin is made up of individuals who both hate and resemble each other (which is why hatred of others is condi-tioned by the most terrible hatred of all, that of self). The result is a curious monotony. If, after hearing so many wretched secrets, confessors were unable to see into people's hearts, they would only have had to say, like Ecclesiastes, 'All things are full of weariness... What has been is what will be, and what has been done is what will be done; and there is nothing new under the sun' (1.8-9).

We must agree with Soloviev that the time has come for 'the justification of the good', which happens to be also the title of one of his books. Not the sickly good of moralism, but the goodness and beauty which is our participation in the fullness of God. A good no longer derived from morality, but from being and communion. Inventiveness, creative energy, originality exist only in the Spirit. Evil is in itself nothing, a bubble. Its chief characteristic is repetition. Within the death and hell surrounding us the emphasis may shift from age to age, or from civilization to civilization – it would be possible to write a history of evil; but there would be nothing left in the historian's mind but pride and despair, that is to say the nothingness brought into being by our misdirected freedom. Nothing would be left but the vertigo of the abyss.

That freedom, which seeks the Spirit of life only to reject and mimic it, can display a certain savage grandeur, a devilish inventiveness. There is a mosaic at Ravenna of the angel Lucifer, very beautiful but infinitely wistful, and infinitely sad, because, although he is at Christ's side, he does not wish to see him. (Which is why sadness, the 'worldly grief' that, according to St Paul, 'produces death', was considered by the great monks to be one of the chief kinds of sin.)

The 19th century was, with notable exceptions, an age of spiritual slumber, when Christianity degenerated into moralism. So little evidence was there of the creative presence of the Holy Spirit that some ardent souls, in their passion for life and beauty, confused him with Lucifer. Baudelaire wrote verses to Satan, and the young Nietzsche, despite being the son of a pastor, or perhaps because of it, spoke of the Trinity of the Father, the Son and Lucifer. Only Léon Bloy understood exactly how to 'discern the spirits': true inspiration is from the Spirit, but he must be liberated from the underworld to which conventional Christian morality has banished him. We are still paying a massive price for the betrayals of the 19th century. But Berdyaev said – and this was borne out in his life – that each Christian receives a special genius from the Spirit, and Simone Weil has called for a 'sanctity which has genius' – something she had already shown she possessed. The Spirit, then, still has his prophets among us. We are discovering that the eucharist, in the words of the ancient Syrian liturgies, is Spirit and Fire.

Blood and Fire

In Christ, God has reunified humanity. From henceforth and without limit of time or space, it is nothing other than the Body of God. That is what Cabasilas meant when he said that people are more truly related to each other in Christ than they are according to the flesh. Carnal kinship leads to death, kinship in Christ to eternity. The blood that springs from the pierced side of Christ, the wine of the eucharist, according to the Fathers, intoxicates us with this great love.

The unity of the Blood answers to the diversity of the Fire; indeed they are inseparable, for the Fire is already burning in the Blood. The Spirit is fire, the blood is red; faith, childish yet profound, understands the mystery, that the blood is the original water – the life of the world – set on fire by the Spirit. So the Blood is not only red but warm; in the Eastern Churches, where all the faithful receive the communion of the blood of Christ, a little hot water, symbolizing the 'fire of the Holy Spirit', is mixed with the wine beforehand.

While we are a single Man in Christ, cleansed and united by the same Blood, each of us is a unique Person in the Holy Spirit. On the day of Pentecost the flames of the Spirit divided, as they have done ever since, each lighting up an irreducible inner being, establishing its freedom, confirming its particular vocation, bringing to life a personal existence. To be a person is to affirm, within and for the sake of communion, something which has never existed before.

So Christians must not only be integrated into Christ's unifying Body. They must also freely express in their lives, according to their own vocations, the power of resurrection that this Body contains.

The Church as the Body of Christ requires an attitude of respect, loyalty and obedience, that obedience to death which we see in Christ; but the Church as the extension of Pentecost calls for courage, imagination, the creative transformation of *eros*, all the conflict experienced by the conscious personality exercising its freedom. But the sole purpose of this conflict is to bring about a communion that is free from the opposing tendencies to individualism and collectivism, self-isolation and fusion. The obedience, ultimately, is the obedience of all to all, so that all may grow together to maturity in love and freedom. Humanity, being one in Christ, is called to the endless diversity of the Spirit.

In its essential nature, that of the womb of a new humanity, the Church is neither a 'superperson' nor the mere aggregation of inspired individuals. It tends at the same time towards unity and diversity. The Trinity, exerting its magnetic attraction, ensures that both the unity and the diversity, the one no less than the other, are unconditional.

We must not think of a person as a cell in a body. Each person, while a member of the one body, is complete in itself. Each one is sufficiently important to the risen Christ to be received by him face to face in his kingdom. There is no question of any comparison; Christ prefers each person. We often think of Christ's love for humanity as if it were egalitarian, repeated over and over again, but such love would be only an abstraction. There are failed monks, stranded between heaven and earth, who talk thus as if God's charity were impersonal. But God certainly prefers the one who is mad with love, who loves one only, to the death. Love is always a preference. And Christ prefers each one. He turns to each to say, You are the one I choose. For him each one is of absolute worth, and absolute means not being part of anything else, containing everything. The saint contains within himself the whole of humanity, the whole universe, because he has within himself that mad love of God for everyone and everything, that love in which alone he himself can exist.

From individual to person

The Body of Christ is not only unity but interchange, by which the 'movement of love' of the Trinity is conveyed to humankind. This movement in which each effaces himself in order to give, is the transition from individual to person, a growing to maturity certainly, but only achieved by means of a succession of death-and-resurrections, in the course of which we are stripped down and recreated. We become unique, escape the repetitive character of sin, only in proportion to our achieving unity. In coming to completion, the personality is shaped by its various tendencies of inclusiveness and discrimination, self-giving and letting be, and by the effects of love and the surrounding creation. No longer do we jealously guard our share of humanity, our own joys, our separateness. We give so that we may bring to life. Giving our life, we receive all lives into ourselves.

But we must beware of wishing to give too quickly, like adolescents, and the militants on the barricades. Such an approach, more than any other, has brought Christianity into disrepute. 'Not everyone who says, Lord, Lord...', not everyone who says, Love, love.

The misshapen and superficial are of no use. Before there can be communion there must first be restoration of balance, inner calm, self-control, the ruling of our natural desires. If we are to love our neighbour we must first love God and his spiritual discipline. Christ can give himself for our food, the Bread of Life, only because he is completely one with the Father.

Joined to the Father through Christ, the heart set at rest, the depth of the heart communing with the depth of God, each of us becomes a human-all-humanity; in the end – an end we never reach, because we are speaking of infinite expansion – we no longer have anything, but we are everything. As Simeon the New Theologian said, 'it is the poor man who loves the human race'.

The individual wishes to possess everything and finds the self empty, turned in on its own nothingness. The person, by the 'poverty of the spirit' which is dis-possession, renounces every-thing and receives everything. Christ says, 'Whatever you renounce, you will receive a hundredfold'. The libertine is even-tually unable to see a woman's secret beauty, the inaccessible loveliness of the person; or, if he does perceive it, he tries to destroy it by treating her as merely a body: 'She is just like all the others.' He multiplies his conquests but can no longer really see a woman's face, or see her body as a face. A chaste man, however, is aware that true beauty is a miracle. Perhaps he will become the saint described by John Climacus, who sang praise to God for the splendour of a woman's body.

If we are bent on power and ambition we see only the appear-ance, see everything in terms of control. But 'blessed are the meek, for they shall inherit the earth.' They already possess it, for they see all things as existing in their own right. If we are both unified and enlarged, we shall discover our true face without even looking for it. Not the face we protect so jealously, the one fashioned for us by the world, our culture, all our cares and suffering. Nor the striking beauty with which we are sometimes graced when we are young. These are merely the material aspect. The real face emanates from the heart, if the heart is enkindled; it arises from the heart as the new Jerusalem will arise from the heart of the God-made-man and from deified humanity. And as the new Jerusalem will transfigure 'the glory and honour of the nations', so the face arising from the heart transfigures the marks of experience, internalizes the beauty of youth.

The power of love has perhaps been best described by Gregory of Nyssa. He was undoubtedly forced to it by the Origenists, whose Christian belief, though profound, was still permeated with the cyclical outlook of the ancient world. According to the Origenists, souls were in the beginning filled with God and with one another, but were surfeited by the experience. Desiring a change, they then chose a state of separation, cold isolation and opposition. A great frost surrounds and penetrates us which is the fallenness of the world. Christ has come to restore everything to its original condition. But what is to stop the threat of surfeit recurring?

Gregory of Nyssa saw the necessity for a decisive break with the ancient cyclical tradition, and conceived instead the notion of a dynamic eternity, an eternity of communion, beginning here on earth. How can we ever have enough? The more God gives himself to me and fills me with his presence, and the more I find him to be new and inexhaustible, the more I am drawn towards him like the bride in the Song of Songs or like the flight of the dove in the never-fading light. The more I come to know him, the more constantly he is to be sought. And in the knowing-unknowing of the neighbour we never come to the end, we can never have too much.

Eternity begins here and now, in our ability to do away with objectification, to see that in Christ the door of clever ignorance which is shut beween me and my neighbour is for ever broken down. In eternity our neighbour is no longer an impersonal object – 'that one' – classified, catalogued, forgotten, but comes to life as profoundly secret, unfathomable as God himself or as I am to myself. Then I am set on a destined path as if entering a land of childhood, knowing very well that, in the words of St Gregory, it will take me all eternity to go 'from beginning to beginning, by way of beginnings without end' (*Commentary on the Song of Songs*, PG,XLIV,941 A). Eternity is a first time, continually renewed.

The miracle of the first time: the first time you realized that this person would be your friend, the first time, in childhood, that you heard that heartrending music, the first time that your child smiled at you, the first time... Then you become used to it. But eternity means becoming unused to it. The more I know God, and my neighbour in the light of God, the more God is revealed, and my neighbour also, as blessedly unknown.

'Whoever would save his life will lose it, and whoever loses his life for my sake will find it.' In Christ I lose my life and receive the Spirit, who is Life itself. In Christ I lose my life, Another receives me and I receive the other. And every other person whom I receive is a wound by which I lose my life, and by which I find it. Christianity is the religion of faces.

Christianity means that God, for us, has become a face and reveals the other as a face. Macarius the Great says that the spiritual person becomes all face, and his face all expression. What can a face that is all expression be but a saving breach in the constricting vastness of the world?

There is nothing more thrilling than interplanetary travel, soon perhaps intergalactic travel. We must explore our prison. But it is a prison without limits. For us the only way out is a face, and first of all the one on our television screens, the face of the cosmonaut wrapped in empty space. The explorer is greater than what he explores, the expression on his face is all that saves us from nothingness. And if his expression should harden, if his face should close, we know that secretly there is an expression that is always welcoming, that the face of Christ is never closed.

The Disciplines of Communion

We can now give an outline of the disciplines of communion.

The first thing, before love is even mentioned, is humility, and what humility becomes when it is exercised towards another person, that is, respect. Respect rejects all self-interested curiosity, all possession of souls. Some people undergo a strict regime of self-denial to free themselves from carnal desire, only to fall prey to a more exquisite desire, that for souls. This must be identified and overcome, especially if there is any pretension to spiritual fatherhood. This art and science is essentially the inspiring of the other person, bringing them to birth, without either entrapping them or attaching them to oneself. Respecting the other as an equal rules out all fusion, all promiscuity, in short, all sexual involvement, of the sort we see in the political or religious preacher whipping up the emotion of the crowd as if he owned it, or in the amorous tendencies of the licensed guru. While irony may be wounding and should be avoided, humour is often necessary for self-deflation. Respect is born of humility, it is the chastity of the whole being. St Isaac the Syrian says, 'When praying to God, imagine you are an ant crawling on the earth... Approach God as if you were a little child ...' (sentence 62). Elsewhere he says it is necessary 'to become as if you were completely unknown, even to your own soul' (sentence 81). It is then that I understand that I am owed nothing, that everything is freely given. Fallen human beings are always expecting everything from others and turning them into scapegoats. At the moment of the fall, Adam, far from repenting, accuses his wife, 'The woman gave me fruit of the tree ...'. In effect he accuses God himself, '... the woman whom *thou* gavest to be with me' (Genesis 3.12). Only if I come to terms with my condition as a creature, my humble place in the order of being, shall I understand that I am owed nothing, since I have been given everything. God gives me existence, and existence is grace. God gives me the world and other people, and when the world allows me a glimpse of its beauty, and when another person allows me a glimpse of his face, my heart swells with gratitude; all is grace. We say exactly the same in the Lord's Prayer when we pray, 'Forgive us our debts, as we forgive our debtors'. If we understand that everything is the gift of God, then all debts are forgiven, and our respect is turned into wonderment.

Spiritual attentiveness, when directed towards some one else, becomes actual astonishment, awakened consciousness, revelation. We experience an intense amazement that other people exist in the warmth of God's light. Think of the peaceful but heartrending, almost intolerable love that we feel when we see a child asleep. How can such beauty exist? How, through the flesh of a man and a woman, could God create this beauty that is neither fleshly nor spiritual, but total, a beauty beyond the reach of any ill-will; that is capable of utter self-abandon, for the child sleeps as only the saints know how to pray. Later, in adolescence, in adulthood, the beauty will disintegrate, heaven and earth will come into conflict. It will be a long struggle to reconcile them. But now, all is given, we see a true face of eternity flowering gently on the darkness, like a water-lily on the water. Perhaps one day the grown-up will be reunited with this first face. Just after a person's death, God often gives him back the face he had as a child, asleep. When we have learnt to die to self in order to be reborn in Christ, we too recover that face; children and wild beasts come up to us. But then our eyes are open.

The training of our consciousness enables us to recover an immediacy of response to anybody's face, however spoilt, haggard, or careworn, and precisely because it is such. God loves this person here and now, in their very ordinariness, their cowardice, their loneliness, their sin. Our consciousness being awakened, the eye of the heart is opened, and we begin to see with the eyes of God.

Then we can put ourselves in the other's place, share the other's experience from within. The other person becomes the image of God for us, not for our delight, but so we can bring to bear the strongest ascetic influence. For nearly always the image is disfigured by the powers of evil; on this new battlefield we must henceforth fight, armed with discernment, love and prayer.

Prayer above all. For the Tradition is unanimous: 'Love is born of prayer', 'Love is the fruit of prayer'. Prayer cleanses the heart of the 'passions' and opens it to the trinitarian expansion. Prayer frees us from indifference and impenetrability, it exposes us to the revelation of the other person, to the other person as revelation.

We must therefore be attentive to others and to God, simultaneously performing service and practising solitude. Every one is pledged to the 'interior monasticism' of which Paul Evdokimov speaks; to be, in his heart of hearts, like a monk, alone with God. There is a famous monastic precept, 'Be all things to all men, weep with those who weep, rejoice with those who rejoice. But in your inmost heart remain alone', before Him, with Him, in Him. And as He is love and the source of love, anyone who, for His sake, separates himself from all finds himself by the same token united to all.

Solitude is a vital discipline both for me and the other person; we must know how to leave each other alone. We do not know how to leave our friends and family alone because we are possessive, continually trying to reconstruct around us the world of our childhood, where we were at the centre.

And solitude is not only physical. Even when we are alone, perhaps then above all, we are inhabited, possessed; not deserts, but public places. The others are in us, and we ourselves are manifold.

So not only is solitude necessary for prayer, but prayer for true solitude. We all have to learn to detach ourselves occasionally – and in any case we all have to sleep – but the saint will in the end bear within himself, even at the heart of the crowd, *utter silence*, the silence of true solitude. Then no one is a stranger to him any more.

Disinterested love

All is summed up in the expression of the Virgin in the 'icons of lovingkindness', for example the Vladimir Mother of God, whose motherhood is so solid, yet transfigured and universal. Today pity is considered demeaning. We confuse it with feeling sorry for some one, whereas it is essentially com-passion, suffering with; unreserved acceptance, a refusal to judge, disinterested love. Disinterested love is perhaps what people need most, now that all love is suspect.

If, as many now believe, the only legitimate expression of *eros* is sexuality, there is no longer any brotherly, sisterly, motherly or fatherly love; only, in the end, incest or (homo)-sexuality. To the Christian this is not the dawn of a liberated humanity, but the degeneration of *eros*. Indeed the old monks were there before Freud; they warned their disciples against the visits of their mother, because, as they said, we do not know what relationship we really have with her. Their tradition was concerned all the time with living in the presence of death. In the end Freud understood; love and death are hand in glove. If we wish to escape from the difficulties of personal life in a universal erotic ecstasy, we do it to forget that we shall die. It is natural that in the East, where death has been conjured away, people should take refuge in a thousand forms of sexual promiscuity. No traveller returned from China, and still intoxicated with its mass excitements, tells us how the dead are treated there. Eroticism, whether between two or three, or among seven hundred million, is a means of escape which reinforces its very futility; was it not Stalin, who knew what he was talking about, who said that death always has the last word?

But if Christ has conquered death, I no longer need any way of escape. In Christ my death is no longer ahead of me but behind me, I can set myself to live and love. Sin, which is regression more than transgression, weighs down and disfigures this love, but the fact remains that love is possible and in its humble way can respond to the love of God that sets us free.

If we cannot abolish this slavery in order to witness to disinterested love, both in relation to our peers and in all 'vertical' relationships symbolizing fatherhood, then everything will shut down. The world will be closed in on itself, and any 'freedom' will be merely slavery in a more subtle form. Now we begin to understand the spiritual reason why incest is taboo; it is in order to make room for love that is disinterested, genuinely personal. A mother is not really a separate person from her son, or a father from his daughter. If marriage were allowed in either case that would be nature swallowing up persons. Where incest is taboo, transcendence intervenes in our daily life.

It is why, more generally, modesty is indispensable. To be acknowledged as a personal presence is to be known by our face, not by our sex. We are fascinated by the sexes because of their very identity, and also because *eros* is so polarized that all personal differences are swallowed up in an overwhelming otherness. Modesty does not abolish the mystery of the sexes; this appears in the face itself and in the gracefulness of the body which shapes the garment and is expressed by it. But there is an established hierarchy, our most 'personalized' frontiers, the face and the hands, taking precedence; and the precise way the clothing fits the body can also reveal, by means of fashions or in spite of them, something of the personality.

Modesty plays a part in all our dealings with the lower orders of creation and is closely linked with the periodic discipline of fasting, which interrupts the relation of violence and murder which we have with the world. Modesty and fasting engender compassion, respect, reverence, the lack of which renders our soul impenetrable.

So married love is possible, the personal encounter that can contain all the immensity of life; and disinterested love is possible, where, because of our immersion in the mystery of God, we can be immersed in the mystery of humanity.

Love is disinterested if it is interested in the being, which is to say the deification, of the other person. 'Let me stay outside, let me be a stone trampled under your feet, my name soon effaced, like the humblest memorials in the Middle Ages, while you go into the banqueting hall!' Where there is prayer like this, disinterested love is present.

Make no mistake, setting out on this path means becoming vulnerable to all the pain of the world. If we did not know that Christ had shed his blood on the cross and uttered his cry of unimaginable despair, we should be crushed beyond recall. Every one who relinquishes the security of a sleepwalking existence is sooner or later mortally wounded by the world's suffering. But because God became man and took this suffering on himself, the way of vulnerability and death becomes for us resurrection. And we can pray and fight for universal salvation: 'My son, I give you this commandment: let mercy always prevail in your balance, till the moment when you feel within yourself the mercy that God shows towards the world' (St Isaac the Syrian, sentence 48).

4

The Search for the 'Place of the Heart'

The temple of the body

We are both person and nature, and the nature itself is also dual, being a synthesis of visible and invisible, each pervading and containing the other. Through the body, we participate in the material and living world; by means of the body, personal existence belongs to the material universe and particularizes it. Cosmic energy is constantly passing through the body, renewing it materially, with the result that the whole of humanity actually possesses a single body, which is the sensible universe. So even in our fallen state, the mystery of human 'consubstantiality', the vocation of each to contain the whole of humanity and contribute to it, is given concrete expression. In our bodies we begin to know the world from within; we have the power to transform it into a living sacrifice or a decaying carcase. Nothing 'spiritual' is left except the form of the body, enduring and perceptible amidst the shifting cosmic forces. Matter is by definition invisible, the result of purely mathematical relations arising from the single intelligence. But out of this play of abstractions, the person, what the Bible calls the 'living soul', makes solid flesh. As the ancient philosophers aptly put it, 'the soul is the form of the body'. What you see is, by definition, not matter, but the soul, the person!

The construction and working of the body are determined by its designed purpose, to be the 'temple of the Spirit'. It is 'bodily' that 'the whole fullness of deity dwells in Christ' (Col. 2.9). Hence the apostle's impassioned plea, 'Do you not know that your body

is a temple of the Holy Spirit?... So glorify God in your body'
(1 Cor. 6.19-20).

Two bodily activities in particular exactly symbolize the fulfilment of its purpose, the sign in each case really embodying the
thing signified: breathing and the beating of the heart.

The Spirit, the Breath of life, can mingle with the breath of
humanity:

Breathing, you invisible poem!
Pure and unceasing exchange between the worldspace
and our own being...
Lone wave, whose
gradual sea I am...
(R.M. Rilke, *Sonnets to Orpheus* 2.1)

The offering of our breath releases us into those immense
spaces; 'Jesus' really means, God sets free, God sets at large.

The pulsing of the blood is the pulsing of the original waters
beneath the breath of the same enkindled Spirit, the pulsing that
sets time and space in motion. As we breathe, the fire in our blood
is continually refuelled. The rhythm of the heart is one of drawing
in and spreading out, purifying and quickening. The heart is the
sun that is still within us, despite the enucleation of the Fall; it is
the sun of the body as the Word is the sun of the worlds. Here again
the correspondence is exact. The heart is the 'high place' become
secret; when we scale mountains, we are looking for the meeting-
point of heaven and earth. When we travel to sun-drenched oceans,
it is to seek enlightenment in our lives from the sun of the heart.

The bowels correspond to the 'bowels of mercy' that in the Bible
are repeatedly, in an almost uterine sense, ascribed to God. The
Spirit surrounds, nourishes, and consoles. Appropriately, in
Semitic languages the word for it is often feminine.

Male *eros* is the reflection in humanity of the mystery of the
Father, who begets and fertilizes. The union between man and
woman is an expression of the union between Christ and his

Church, between the creating Word and the earth which he recreates. And the earth is not merely passive, for she must freely consent, in the person of a woman, to receive her Redeemer.

Hence the observation of Basil Rozanov, a Russian religious philosopher at the beginning of the century, famous for his intuitive and poetic writings about marriage, who said that *eros*, not only the spiritual state but its sexual expression, has taken on a fundamentally religious meaning. 'It is the atheist,' he says, 'who has no understanding of the flesh.' 'The sexual act, in its deepest meaning, which is now completely forgotten, is precisely the act by which we do not destroy chastity, but on the contrary acquire it.' And after discussing the deep significance and unmistakable realness of biblical circumcision, Rozanov concludes, 'All thinking about sex made people think about God; it soon lost the cruel sensuality with which we are so familiar, and was dissolved in an awareness of the divine; this is where the Lord takes possession of me.'

'O Lord our God, who hast honoured man with thine image; who hast endowed him with a reasonable soul and a comely body, the body being subject to the soul; who hast placed the head in the highest place and disposed in it the chief part of the senses, so that they are in harmony with each other...', so reads the Byzantine prayer at the tonsure, during the rite of baptism, which symbolizes, by the cutting of several locks of hair, the offering to God of the human being as possessing reason and conscience. The head being bound to the heart, which itself controls and elevates the *eros*, is therefore hand in glove with the 'reasonable soul' which harmonizes the senses and reflects the divine Reason, the Word or Wisdom of God. 'Reason, that is man,' as a Father of the Church said (Basil, *The Creation of Man*, 7,PG,XXX,17C). All the dimensions that humanism has given to reason – intellectual rigour, clarity, discipline, methodical study – are here confirmed, enlarged and transfigured. By reason, says another Father, humanity 'crosses the seas, visits the heavens with the eye of the spirit, and contemplates the courses, distances and sizes of the stars... By science and discovery he is triumphant... Man is master of everything' (Nemesius of Emesa, *On Human Nature*, I,PG,XL,533A,B).

By reason humankind is mediator and saviour of the universe, and the means of its self-expression; all humanity's scientific research and technological mastery belongs to that exalted role. By reason, humankind is king, but the human being must also become priest, for the Greek word *logikos*, 'logic', which we translate as reasonable, also means resembling the Logos, the Word and Wisdom of God. So reason is both scientific investigation and the attainment of Wisdom. Today, for example, as biologists study living organisms, they see at work an Intelligence whose processes human intelligence can do no more than imitate, even in its most sophisticated activities, such as in information technology. And the only possible explanation of the interplay of systems and events which make up the history of the world is that this intelligence is personal.

Heidegger identified a conflict between the analytical study of creation and the impulse to rejoice in it, but this opposition is now abolished in favour of a science inspired by worship, and worship continually enriched by science. It is through all its rational activity as king of creation that humankind must accomplish its offering as priest.

The 'heart-spirit'

So there has grown within the rich Christian tradition the idea of *integrated knowledge*, which assumes the necessity of reason, but in conjunction with the other faculties and senses, such as willpower, love, and the awareness of beauty. Integrated knowledge is knowledge in faith; it combines human nature in a personal movement of encounter and communion. By this communion the fullness of the godhead is communicated to human nature, reaching the very ground of the being, what the Fathers called the 'earth of the body'; in other words, by way of the body, the earth itself. The whole person thus becomes a vehicle of worship, in a transition so peremptory and sudden as to seem almost physical. The Fathers speak of 'feeling God' as well as of knowing him. While the body, being grafted by baptism on to the deifying body of Christ, is nourished in its depths by the energy of the Resurrection, the consciousness roams about 'committing adultery with idols'. It is then that the great spiritual teachers of the Eastern Church recommend a simple and basic exercise: 'incorporate the incorporeal in the corporeal', attend carefully and thankfully to the humblest sensations, breathing, walking, eating. A poet has said that only a purified soul can appreciate the scent of the rose. The essence of the world is holiness, and we bear holiness in our bodies. It is important that our hearts are aware of it.

Integrated knowledge is therefore a faculty of the whole person, created in order to become a sanctuary of God's presence in the midst of the world. But the human person, like a good musician, or a good musical instrument, must be made ready, tightened and stretched, tuned to resonate with the song of being. The focus of this activity is called, in line with the biblical and Christian tra-dition, the 'heart-spirit'. Some people, starting from St Paul's threefold division – body, soul and spirit – have tended to emphasize the last; the soul then means the mind, and the spirit the openness of the person to the Holy Spirit (when St Paul speaks of the spirit, it is often hard to tell whether he means the human spirit, or God's). Others, following biblical symbolism directly, have laid more emphasis on the heart. When people finally realized that these were two ways of saying the same thing, they used the expression 'heart-spirit'.

Throughout the Bible, but especially in the earlier, less sophisti-cated books, the heart is not merely the bodily seat of the emotions, but the centre, symbolic but real, of the person, the place where all the faculties are combined, and where the spiritual combat is fought. It is the inmost self, so that sin consists in the heart's being at variance with the lips. It is the origin of the feelings, will-power, and passion, the last being transformable into com-passion. A joyful person is said to be 'of good heart'; in sadness the heart is 'sick'. And above all, the heart is the place of intelligence, both of its contemplative roots and of its mature expression. So it stands for the person, the place where nature opens upon the irreducible fathomlessness of personal existence. Therefore it is utterly mysterious; only God 'knows the secrets of the heart' (Psalm 44.21). And so the 'bottom of the heart' is the place where we encounter God, where we open or shut to the one who 'stands at the door', begging for love. Rejection of God, withdrawing into oneself, are called in the Bible 'hardness of heart'. The faithful heart, on the contrary, is 'fixed' on God.

That is why God, using our experiences, cultivates our hearts like a good ploughman, breaking up the hard dry earth to let in water and seed. God is 'near to the broken-hearted' (Psalm 34.18). And the prophet, announcing the end of all things, which for us is the coming of Christ, describes both the heart and the spirit as being opened to the Holy Spirit: 'A new heart I will give you, and a new spirit I will put within you; I will take out of your flesh the heart of stone and give you a heart of flesh. And I will put my spirit within you ...' (Ezekiel 34.26-27).

In the New Testament this unveiling of the 'hidden man of the heart' is dramatically accomplished. The light shed upon our hearts by the incarnate Word chases out the ravages inflicted there by the powers of evil. If we reject the light, our heart becomes 'double', and is given over to the devil who is called 'legion'. From the heart arise 'thoughts' – the seeds of passions – which lead us to 'pride, foolishness' (Mark 7.21). Only by faith, only by a thorough 'turning round' can we receive a 'new heart' in Christ. Then are we filled in the depth of our being with all the fullness of God. But the baptismal 'enlightenment' is buried in the unconscious. The Christian Tradition tells us to 'seek the place of the heart'.

A lifegiving discipline

Our whole spiritual progress is a 'search for the place of the heart'. Little by little, the conscious self frees itself from idols, strips away the dead layers and illusions, and 'descends', like Psyche holding a lighted lamp, into the dark crypt of the heart. Sanctuary, crypt and tomb become the bridal chamber; the 'heart-spirit' is remade in the fire of grace, it trembles with joy, it bursts into flames, the world and humanity are in it, and already Christ comes again in glory.

This lifegiving discipline is that of the Beatitudes: self-denial, love in action, tears of grief and wonderment dissolving the heart of stone. *Eros* is not quenched – St John Climacus says we must love God with all our *eros* – but becomes intelligent and voluntary, is transformed into awakening, adoration and acceptance. This taking to flight is accomplished, as the Fathers say, with the two wings of free will and grace. But our will develops naturally in unison with our growth in Christ, and cooperates in freeing us from death in its manifold forms, and allowing the divine life to penetrate us and restore our true nature.

In the Eastern Church, not surprisingly, the commonest spiritual technique is the repetition of the Name of Jesus in time with the breathing. The Name itself is a quasi-sacrament of the presence, indicating both the Word by whom everything exists and the Risen Lord by whom creation can be restored to holiness. As the Name is repeated, 'custody of the heart' becomes easier; when a 'thought', in the Gospel sense, arises from the subconscious, it is intercepted by the Name before it can become an obsession, and stripped of any demonic associations; the energy thus released is transformed into a 'clothing' of the same Name. As an angler studies the surface of the water, the spiritual person keeps watch in the silence of the night, detecting thoughts and catching them. Thus 'the discipline of the soul renders it humble and cleanses it of the movements of the passions, transforming them into movements of contemplation'

(St Isaac the Syrian, sentence 40). Little by little the invocation pervades the unconscious, and continues even during sleep. The sleeper is visited by luminous, sometimes prophetic, dreams. There is actually less need for sleep. Deep sleep, the paradoxical state in which we are unconscious and at the same time energetically dreaming, is, as we know, essential for our well-being. But the invocation somehow turns it into a conscious state, a *true dream* by which the perception of beings and things is freed from devilish hallucinations to reveal the 'forms of light' hidden beneath.

If prayer is 'wholehearted', the moment comes when by repetition of the Name the heart is thoroughly set alight, prayer enters the very pulsing of the blood. Then worship becomes spontaneous, truly corresponding to the nature of humanity (and of the universe); a person no longer prays, but is prayer. 'He is drunk with love as with wine,' says St Isaac (sentence 40).

Transfiguration

We were created naked but clothed with light, light that shone upon the world to transfigure it. But at the Fall God clothed us with 'garments of skins' (Genesis 3.21) to protect us from a world become hostile. And now, in our fallen state, our own skin has become a barrier setting us apart from the universe, and signalling that the organism hidden within is a machine for consuming everything outside until its inevitable death. And the predatory theme is reinforced by the fact that all our clothing, animal or vegetable, is dead. It protects us from nature and from our own nature. We alternate between this envelope of dead skins, which is impervious to the life of the cosmos, and the brief ecstasy of the living skin, which has nothing to do with eternity but serves, almost impersonally, to perpetuate the species.

However, our skin is still an ideal of beauty and a reminder of paradise. When we bare it to the wind and the sea we are seeking the *eros* of the child in paradise; *eros* not of the sexual organs but of the whole skin. And in the early days of the hippie movement there was a recovery of the ancient significance of clothing as the 'cosmization' of humanity, in both senses of *cosmos*, meaning universal order and finery; in clothing ourselves, we put on the world as an ornament.

Meanwhile everything is still ambiguous; 'cosmization' is not deification, and our beaches in summer are crowded, to adapt a Gospel expression, with sepulchres not whited but tanned!

Only in Christ can we secretly recover our garment of light, when we put on his transfigured humanity. This secret light can shine through the 'garments of skins' and, for a moment, or more lastingly, transform the chaos around us into cosmos. This sometimes happens with true love, when we experience, in Rozanov's words, 'innocence, chastity, holiness of the skin...without which tenderness, passion or love would be inconceivable'. In such a love, the transfiguration of the world is already beginning, the garments of skins are becoming the garments of light.

It happens most of all when someone achieves holiness. There are plenty of examples in Christian hagiography of the transfiguration of the senses and body, but the most significant is certainly St Seraphim of Sarov. After living for a long time under a rule of silence, Seraphim seemed animated directly by the Spirit; he prayed continuously; thousands of visitors came to him; he read hearts and prophesied and healed souls and bodies. One day in the winter of 1831 he was in the forest talking to a young layman, Motovilov, whom he had cured, and whose spiritual father he had become. Motovilov, in a state of mental anguish, asked the old monk how to discern the presence of the Holy Spirit. Seeing that mere words would have no effect, Seraphim instantly appeared before him transfigured, and made him come into the light.

'We are both in the fullness of the Holy Spirit. Why are you not looking at me?'

'I cannot, Father. Lightning is flashing from your eyes. Your face is brighter than the sun.'

'Do not be afraid. You are shining as brightly as I. You are also now in the fullness of the Holy Spirit, otherwise you would be unable to see me... Have the courage to look at me. God is with us.'

'I looked at him, and a still greater fear seized me. Imagine someone who is talking to you – and his face appears like the sun at midday. You see his lips moving and the expression of his eyes changing, you hear the sound of his voice, you feel his hands gripping you by the shoulders, but at the same time you see neither his hands, nor his body, nor yours, only a brilliance which spreads all around, to a distance of several yards, lighting up the snow which was settling on the grass and falling gently on the great staretz and on me.'

Then St Seraphim, by a series of questions, makes Motovilov undertake a kind of exploration of his new state, bringing him to acknowledge that he feels 'extraordinarily well', and that he is filled 'with an inexpressible silence and peace'. And besides peace, gentleness, joy, warmth and fragrance. 'Years ago, when I went dancing, before I left for the ball, my mother would sprinkle me with scents that she used to buy in the best shops... but their smell could not be compared with these spices.' As a result of Seraphim's teaching, the Spirit enlightened not only the soul but the body, making it impervious to cold and transfiguring even the sense of smell, the most primitive of the senses, bound to the mysterious smell of the earth.

'And so it must be,' the saint concluded. 'Divine grace dwells in our lowest depths, in our hearts. As the Lord has said, the Kingdom of Heaven is within you. By Kingdom of Heaven he means the grace of the Holy Spirit. It is within us at this moment, warming us, enlightening us, rejoicing our senses and filling our heart with joy."'

And these are not Hindus who are having this transcendental experience, but Christians; they are 'bearers of the Spirit' only to the degree they remain 'bearers of the Cross', utterly dedicated to the unlimited vulnerability of personal love.

5

The Destiny of *Eros*

Eroticism, passion and the Gospel

Today, partly as a result of daring experimentation, but mostly because of a willingness to go along with fashion, sex seems to be everywhere. The mass media, advertising, and a general inclination to rebelliousness, have together encouraged the spread of a sub-Freudian culture which, combined with Marxist fantasies, has even lost the awareness of death which Freud had recovered. The horror of 'repression', the shallow sensation-seeking demanded by our jaded nerves and imagination, seem to arise from a whole mass of disappointments.

The first disappointment is work, which is so often mechanical, repetitive and apparently purposeless; and although it is less laborious than it used to be, thanks to the advance of technology, it causes more nervous tension, for which sex seems to be the only relief. For many people in a technological society, the only real bit of nature they are ever going to encounter is the body of another person.

Ultimately everything is a disappointment, because of people's extreme isolation and the nihilism implicit in their outlook on life. The last approach to holiness, or other people, that is left to them, is through erotic experience. When the young revolutionaries realize that their Utopia is unattainable, they are left with their facile sexual revolution, their intoxication with 'freedom', their experience of ecstasy through orgy, which they think they are the first to discover. The 'communes' with their sexual promiscuity are a pathetic and infantile attempt to achieve fusion, to escape from loneliness and death, from the loneliness of death.

With the constant talk about sex, the erotic fantasies that invade our minds, and the laboriousness of having to act them out, and the 'permissiveness' which results from the pressure to conform or to rebel, everything eventually loses its meaning. And because of this meaninglessness, arousal becomes even more important, inasmuch as, for the time being, sex seems to be selling well and to be making other things sell. Whence the ever more violent and more mechanical character of modern eroticism, a sign in itself of how feeble we have become in our capacity for true feeling. There are signs of impotence and frigidity. In fact, those who really know about *eros* scarcely talk about it. Mediterranean people, for example, are more modest than those of the North. There are also signs of things falling apart. We may be less repressed, but we are also less integrated, even within the personality, where it is becoming harder to trace any consistent principle.

But why stop at sex? Leaving the intellectuals to their exercises, we find that ordinary people have quite a different preoccupation: passion, or 'romance'. Denis de Rougemont, in *Love and the West*, a seminal book of our time, says that one of the most enduring myths is that of Tristram and Iseult, even, or especially, among people who have never actually heard of them. Rougemont's theory is that romantic love is born of the opposition between the Christian affirmation of the person and the deep-rooted persistence, in the Christian world, of a purely functional idea of marriage. For a very long time marriages were arranged irrespective of love, to ensure the continuity of the line. But the person, now awakened to the necessity of free choice, sought love outside marriage; so came about the romantic passion of the troubadour or the knight for his lady. We can go further and demonstrate that the first form of entirely personal love in Western history was the spiritual friendship between men and women *who had renounced marriage*, such as the spiritual love displayed by St Boniface in his letters to

St Lioba. We must remember the context: Merovingian society, brutal to the point of cruelty, where people married for purely biological reasons and sought carnal diversion in rape and adultery. Monks and nuns exerted an immense effort to rescue personal existence from all this frenzy of 'flesh and blood'. Then they were able amongst themselves to use the language of genuine love. But the flesh was still so violent that personal love seemed incapable of finding expression through the body.

In any case, romantic love, because it is conceived in absolute terms, without any real personal involvement, does not lend itself to incarnation; as Denis de Rougemont ironically says, we cannot imagine Iseult as Mrs Tristram. In romantic passion, love is coupled inextricably with its absolute opposite, suffering. For a brief moment the sublime creature fulfils our hope, then comes the inevitable disillusionment; the whole thing turns out to be a fabrication, and when the object of our adoration is revealed in the light of day as quite ordinary we wake up indifferent, even frozen. It is common knowledge that romantic passion grows and dies like a disease. And when it is dead, we ask what happened; we no longer know. 'How could you be faithful, since you are incapable of grasping the meaning of any life but your own? I wonder how you think of me, and whether you ever do think of me otherwise than in images of your own. I have searched your notebook in vain for some of my mannerisms. Apart from the twitch in my lip, nothing comes to life. You have never been interested in me as myself, only as you choose to see me. Has it ever occurred to you that I might have a life distinct from you?' (Pierre Emmanuel, *Because I love you.*)

True love is neither impersonal sex nor passion as an end in itself. *Eros* must be subordinate to affection; love desires the salvation of the other, but knows that reciprocal love can be the means of the salvation of both. Christ has brought us back to the original marriage in Eden, repeating exactly what was spoken by the creative Word, that the man and the woman should be 'one flesh'.

True marriage, not the social institution but the *mystery*, has been possible ever since. In Christ we can overcome 'hardness of heart' and serve an apprenticeship of faithfulness to the image of God, who has always been faithful, saying yes to us, even when we were rejecting him. From that moment onwards the deep relationship of man and woman in marriage has been governed by forgiveness, the love that is stronger than death. At the same time, we can no longer say, as the discipline of the Old Covenant insisted, that it is not good for man to be alone. For, in the communion of the Church, the dangers of solitude are overcome, celibacy can be a calling of prayer and service, a sign of the world to come. Beside marriage, and deeply related to it, is the monastic way, also leading to the ful-filment of *eros*.

Monks and martyrs

When the emperor was converted, and the ever-present danger of martyrdom disappeared, monasticism arose to take its place. There was a fear that Christianity would be secularized, that, as it stood, it would become the cement of an earthly city. Monasticism was the revolt against all compromise.

Monasticism, in its early form, was a steep path, that of 'the violent, who take the kingdom of heaven by force'. Utter obedi-ence to the Gospel demands the rejection of conformity and ambi-guity. For the monk, only God is wholly interesting. To people busy with the affairs of this world, the monk is a marginal figure, mad, an outlaw; indeed he does try to escape the law by going beyond it, by living that life of the Spirit of whom we know not 'whence it comes or whither it goes'.

Some Fathers have called monasticism a 'holy aberration'. If the persecution of Christians actually began again, there would no longer be any good reason for institutionalized monasticism to exist; there would only be celibacy practised within clandestine worshipping communities, who would sometimes be called to martyrdom. That was the situation during the three first centuries A.D.; and the cult of the saints, which began with the sub-apostolic period, was initially the cult of the martyrs.

We must understand what martyrdom means in Christianity. It is not only the witness, before earthly judges, of the sole divinity of Christ; it is the mystical state par excellence. The martyr is not an ascetic, but a person of total faith. A young Christian woman, brought pregnant into the Roman prisons, groaned when her child was born. 'What will you say when you are thrown to the beasts?' a gaoler mocked. But she replied, 'Then there will be someone else within me who will suffer for me'. If at the very moment of falling headlong into suffering, the martyr holds to the Crucified and Risen Lord with all the force of his suffering, and indeed with all the violence of the fall itself, he is pervaded by the power of the resurrection and the sensation of joy. St Ignatius of Antioch said – and testified by his own death – 'He is ground into fine flour by the lions' teeth', and becomes 'the purest bread'; in some way he becomes the eucharist. And when the political situation changes and martyrdom is temporarily abolished, then the monk appears, who in another way, according to an old saying, 'gives his blood and receives the Spirit'.

Like the witness of the martyr, that of the monk is a thorn in the flesh of the world, salt in the wound – 'You are the salt of the earth' – which prevents history from being closed in upon itself. In him the End is present here and now, and the world is transformed into a 'burning bush'.

At certain moments in history, the fullness of the gospel witness passes from the martyr to the monk. In Russia, for example, all organized monastic life disappeared between the wars. But there were many martyrs and we know that they prayed for their tormentors. Today most of the monasteries which had been reopened just after the war have been closed again. But there is evidence that there are monks living in secret, undergoing a new kind of martyrdom, which consists of humiliation and oppression, the 'martyrdom of life'. They live under vows, they are occupied in prayer, they do not marry.

The monk does not marry because he actually wishes to hasten time, to replace the birth of others, into time, with the birth of self, into eternity. It is good to have children, because each is a person wanted by God and because the Kingdom will not come before the predetermined number of the elect has been made up (elect, that is, not for their own sake, but in order to work for the salvation of the world). But abstention from marriage for the sake of God is a clearer announcement of the Kingdom, a refusal to settle down in history and in the continuation of the species. It is to consume the seed of time within oneself, instead of allowing it to spread.

And we see something similar in true love between a man and a woman: they do not come together in order to have children, but because they love each other, and their love, without further delay, would go on to transfigure the universe. But delay there must be.

Monasticism, the fulfilment of eros

Like John lying on his Master's breast at the Last Supper, and later, in old age, seeing the dazzling face of the Lord of the universe, the monk is fascinated by the incomparable beauty of the Risen Christ. In him *eros* is altogether robed in the beauty of love and light, all the more beautiful because it shines through the disfigurement of the Passion and the Cross. There is no more room here for another expression of *eros*; the Disfigured and the Transfigured Christ are distinct and the same; here the monk sees the extent of the 'mad love' of God for him and for all, and what other love could he need?

We must love God with all the strength of *eros*. St John Climacus said that we must love him as we should a lover or spouse. The monk burning with such love becomes 'apostolic'; knowing God with all his being he speaks of him as of right. His is not armchair theology, acquired from books, but true theology learned in pure prayer. He speaks of God like some one describing his travels. It is a journey he has made and paid for with his blood. These excellent monks make their pilgrimage into the vastness of God, in order to return to us with faces shining like the face of Moses when he came down from Sinai. Without them the Church would be dying. The Church needs martyrs and monks for her health.

In a society in love with wisdom as well as power we should expect to find not only laboratories for scientific research, but spiritual laboratories dedicated to the more important 'research into God'. Eventually we see that squabbling about the existence of God is ridiculous. Better to pay close attention to those who know God from experience, whose humanity is evidently not degraded, but rather enhanced, by their faith and the integrated knowledge which results from it.

We need spiritual people who can be our spiritual fathers. We have been orphans for too long. We have turned the cure of souls into an crude form of psychoanalysis. We also need the contemplatives who practise their 'art of arts and science of sciences', monks able to discern spirits and to enter deep into the 'heart' (which is rather deeper than the unconscious of the psychoanalysts), experts in the strategy of unseen combat. Monks are indispensable!

Obedience, chastity, poverty

The traditional monastic vows make it possible to love God 'with all your heart, with all your soul and with all your mind'.

Obedience sets freedom free by crucifying the love of self. The person who is committed in all confidence, in sheer faith even, to a 'father' who is further advanced along the path of liberation, overcomes self-importance, breaks the hold of the 'passions', and achieves detachment and inner peace, being lifted up in prayer and carried into the communion of saints. Obedience annihilates self-worship, which is the root of all idolatry; it learns to submit to all life in order to magnify it; in other words it teaches the monk to become a 'father' in his turn.

Poverty, or simplicity of life, together with obedience, exposes us to God's power; to humble ourselves at God's hands is to allow him to recreate us. At every moment I receive myself from him, I receive everything, and everything is freely given. Poverty is the other face of celebration. The layman committed to the world can cultivate an inner poverty, and so overcome the worship of wealth, refusing to take seriously the obsession with producing and consuming. Thus the foundation is laid for Paul Evdokimov's world-wide economy based on sharing, and directed towards communion by means of the true miracle of the loaves: the eucharist.

Chastity is a rich and profound element in the Tradition of the early Church, as valid for the married person as for the monk. Chastity signifies harmony, inner peace, self-restraint, integrity. Chastity is to be found where *eros*, the natural life force, is really integrated into the person. Self-abandonment to the blind movement of *eros* results in *disintegration*. And to kill *eros* without restoring it to new life in the Spirit engenders a somewhat inquisitorial hard-heartedness, a peculiarly monastic vice. But if we can turn it into the immensity of personal love, then the driving force of our life becomes the celebration of an encounter, a hymn to tenderness; love for the ultimate beauty of Christ, perhaps, as he reveals the secret of all faces, the gentleness of the whole created being. We think of St Teresa, in the cloister of Avila, dancing for sheer joy, and accompanying herself on the tambourine. It might also be, and there is no contradiction, the face of the beloved causing the poet to exclaim, in words so commonplace but so true:

'How beautiful is the world, beloved,
how beautiful is the world!'

Obedient, poor, chaste, the monk becomes the world's watchman. The Patriarch Justinian, giving a rule to the monks of the Romanian Church in 1953, enjoined them 'to pray for those who do not know how to pray, or cannot, or will not'. Similarly, a monk of Athos said to a passing guest, during the almost interminable night offices, 'Truly we are obliged to conquer all the sleep of the world.'

Such are the violent who take the Kingdom by force; they see all things in the light of the coming Christ, and thus hasten his coming.

Nevertheless, a true monk is not at all indifferent to feminine beauty, in its essential, or what we might call its 'paracletic' aspect, from the name of the Paraclete, the Spirit, the 'comforter'. On Athos, for instance, nothing feminine is allowed, but everywhere, at the heart of every monastery, we find the icon of the Mother of God, and Athos is often called the Virgin's Garden. So by the mediation of the most feminine face, *eros* ascends towards eternity. In the same way a spiritual friendship can play a precious part in a life dedicated to adoration. But then,

> *Love what are love's worthiest, were all known;*
> *World's loveliest – men's selves. Self flashes off frame and face.*
> *What do then? how meet beauty? merely meet it; own,*
> *Home at heart, heaven's sweet gift; then leave, let that alone.*
> *Yea, with that though, wish all, God's better beauty, grace.*

(Gerard Manley Hopkins, *To what serves mortal beauty?*)

The nuptial way

It is entirely fitting that the first revelation of the consubstantiality, the unity, of human nature, in the Bible should be in terms of marriage: 'This at last is bone of my bones and flesh of my flesh,' says the man when God brings the woman before him. And Genesis adds this comment on what marriage actually entails: 'Therefore a man leaves his father and mother and cleaves to his wife, and they become one flesh,' words that Christ was to repeat in the Gospel. Thus the love of the man and woman is original, paradisal, established in its glory before sin was even thought of: 'And the man and his wife were both naked, and were not ashamed' (Genesis 2.23-25). Paradise is the home of the couple, not the monk.

The condition of banishment has profoundly affected the relationship between man and woman. They have been swept along in the impersonal rush of *eros*, painfully seeking each other, finding each other for a moment, only to lose each other again; or never meeting at all.

Paul Evdomikov, in his invaluable meditation on human love, takes the question God addressed to Adam in paradise, when paradise was already lost – 'Where are you?' – and applies it symbolically to man and woman. Throughout the course of history, he writes, man and woman call to each other, 'Where are you?', being attracted and repelled in succession. Maryse Choisy has spoken of the 'war of the sexes', which is a subject in itself. Society has not always been patriarchal; man has not always dominated woman. Matriarchy has existed in history and prehistory, surviving till the 18th century in certain districts of France where society was semi-nomadic. Polyandry was practised in Tibet until modern times, actually being considered a safe method of birth control. Thinking as we do of the feminine as belonging more to the vegetable world, which accumulates energy, and the masculine to the animal world, which expends it, we sense, not so much the domination of one side by the other, as a complex interplay of forces pulling this way and that. In many ancient traditions, and more recently in tantrism, which arose in India when patriarchy was at its height, the approach to the divine was by way of symbolism that was both cosmic and feminine (not only Mother Earth, but Mother God) and there was a feminine priesthood.

The greater strength of the man is opposed by the woman's biological tenacity. Sexually, the man is bent on instant gratification, the woman on lasting enjoyment. She serves the male, but at the same time gives birth to and infantilizes him, her ultimate service being to the species. The man, meanwhile, is always tempted to lose himself on the breast of the great cosmic mother.

It is in the mystical union between Christ and the Church that the Christian seeks the reconciliation of man and woman, of masculine and feminine, of *eros* and the person. Christianity, although at times distorted by the surrounding culture, has always asserted the transcendence of the person; insisted that the man and the woman, since they are persons, are much more than equals; they are each of absolute worth. That is what St Paul meant when he wrote that, in Christ, 'there is neither male nor female' (Galatians 3.28).

Seen from this point of view, true marriage, which is not sociological but sacramental – 'a great mystery', according to the Apostle – can be no threat, as we have said, to true chastity.

At the first Ecumenical Council in Nicaea, there was some suggestion that marriage was incompatible with the priesthood because sexual relations are a cause of impurity. It must be strongly emphasized that, from the beginnings of Christianity, this had *never* been seen as a problem. The Apostle Peter himself was married, and Clement of Alexandria, quoting an ancient source, describes the married love of the Apostle and his wife as reaching its fulfilment at the moment of martyrdom. At the end of his life St Paul, who tended towards monasticism, and had chosen to remain celibate in expectation of the Lord's imminent return, was asked to decide the organization of the communities which he had founded; he said only that the bishop (the word then denoted the equivalent of the modern priest as well as bishop) should be 'the husband of one wife'. This requirement was not moral, but mystical; for in the early Church, as in the Orthodox Church today, a remarried widower could not be admitted to the priesthood. The faithfulness of the priest to one woman only, even beyond death, was the necessary reflection of the absolute faithfulness of God.

In reaction to the pansexualism of some pagan cults, a dualist, fundamentally Manichean, outlook became widespread, and at the same time there was a revival of an Old Testament distinction between pure and impure; meanwhile the priesthood had evolved into a clerical caste. These all combined to raise the question, at the Council of Nicaea, of the purity, or otherwise, of marriage. It was a famous Egyptian monk, Paphnutius, speaking from experience of ascetic chastity, who forcibly reminded the Council that marriage is chaste, and therefore perfectly consistent with the exercise of the priesthood.

In the Tradition of the undivided Church, the distinction between the monastic and married states did not at all coincide with that between priests and laity. It was quite normal for laymen to seek fulfilment in celibacy. Down to Carolingian times, monks in the West were almost all laymen, and in the East, with a few exceptions, it remains true today. There are even monastic communities without a priest at all; one has to come in for the eucharist on feasts and Sundays, and the rest of the time the monks sing the offices as lay people, with a few special rules, are entitled to do. Just as a layman can be called to celibacy, a married man can equally well be called to the priesthood, which is quite usual in the East. We can well understand that a priest might remain celibate, after the example of St Paul, in order to be more available for his apostolic work. It is evidence of love's inventiveness. And here we see a characteristic feature of the Eastern experience of priesthood: the business of the Church is to choose the best people to be priests, whether they are celibate or married. The essential thing is to avoid opposition; celibacy is not the preserve of the clergy, for the laity also have the right to commit themselves whole-heartedly; nor is it easy to see how marriage, since it is a sacrament, and all the sacraments are like so many rays from the one eucharistic sun, could be incompatible with the sacrament of Holy Order. Perhaps this seems such an intractable problem in the Catholic Church not only because of long historical conditioning but also because the atmosphere of the world in which it finds itself is unfavourable to any spiritual discipline; true chastity cannot be conceived of as attractive to all. The result is that the Church has come to view the monastic way of life as superior. Meanwhile, clean counter to this, the delirious pursuit of fulfilment through sexual 'freedom' plays havoc with some of the clergy, many of whom, still, are all the more vulnerable for having been 'set apart' much too young, in accordance with an individualistic and sentimental understanding of 'vocation', with the result that they experience the crisis of adolescence in their forties or fifties.

Marriage is chaste because it integrates the erotic relationship of the two persons into their communion within the Church; as their mutual love is expressed through their complementary natures, each gives the other to the world. For nine centuries there was no distinctive rite of marriage for Christians. The couple would marry, then go together to communion. For a man and a woman whose life is rooted in Christ, their love is something they have to discover, renew, provide with a face – each giving it the face of the other, and both giving it the faces of their children. They do not have to invent it; it existed before them, it brought them together; it is the love of God for the world, of God for the human race, of Christ for his Church. According to the usual account the woman was born during the man's 'sleep', but the Greek of the Septuagint is more accurately translated 'ecstasy'. In the same way the death of Christ on the Cross is an 'ecstasy' which gives birth to the new humanity. This ecstasy of the Crucified is the basis of all human love. Every true love, even far beyond the visible borders of the Church, wittingly or unwittingly retraces this ecstasy. The unwitting love will wear itself out, unless death comes first, for 'love is a sickness full of woes'. But the love that knows will be enabled to draw from the inexhaustible ecstasy of Christ. From his pierced side flow the water of baptism and the blood of the eucharist. From the gaping wound of his torment the Spirit springs. When human love seems to be running dry, we need only bore down into the limitless reserves of divine-human love. After repentance, forgiveness, the 'wilderness' of unreciprocated trust, the other is suddenly restored to us; our amazement and gratitude deepen as our faithfulness becomes, in the Spirit, an opportunity for renewal. As a result, again and again we experience between us not just the transitory flights of passion but peace, joy, mutual trust – sure evidence of the 'great mystery'.

So in the discipline of marriage there are three golden rules.

The first is that hindrances must be internalized, not conjured away. Love will endure, will avoid sinking into promiscuity or fatigue, only if its way is peppered with obstacles. In a true marriage, these do not disappear, they are internalized. They remain as obstinate reminders that the other is a person in his or her own right; all too close, perhaps, but nevertheless a neighbour. 'One flesh' means one life; not fusion, but communion; they must know how to stay two. Each must be aware of the other's distinct existence, just as real, just as profound; mysterious, not in its opaqueness, which can all too easily provoke hatred, but in its very transparency.

The second rule is that we must refuse to objectify *eros*. After the reticence of Victorian times, Western society is now obsessed with the 'arts of love'. If love is a language, by all means let us learn to speak it. But what good is that if there is nothing left to say to each other, if we are nothing more than smoothly functioning machines? Rejecting the wanderings of fantasy on one hand and mechanical sex on the other; balancing the other person's need for attention with our own wish to live life to the full – that is a discipline which hardly anybody finds attractive.

The third rule is that human love is fulfilled and transcended in joint service. A couple who are completely wrapped up in each other are lost. The only choice they have is between mutual destruction and combined creation, in that general impetus of service and life, or service to life, which is the distinguishing mark of the Church. This is clearly exemplified in the married clergy of the undivided Church, and of the Orthodox today, where the priesthood is, in a sense, assumed not by the man alone, but by the couple.

And here arises the mystery which is at the heart of the family: the child. 'For this reason I bow my knees before the Father, from whom every *family* in heaven and on earth is named' (Ephesians 3.14-15). From a properly Christian point of view, the end of marriage is procreation. True love has no end; it is its own justification. But that means it cannot be fruitful except in the fruits of joint service and effort, the joint welcoming of others, or bringing children 'into the world'. How few couples really bring their children into the world! How many are wrapped up in them, devouring them with their sweaty adoration, till the children, with pitiless cruelty, deliver themselves from that sterile family womb! How many adults seek the meaning of life in their children, instead of transmitting it to them! They are servants of the species, not of the person. Truly bringing children into the world means knowing how to give them not only life, but the example of creative service; it means accepting the fate of the bark which surrounds the bud, giving necessary protection, opening little by little, until it is no longer needed. It means making of the family and household the 'little Church' of which St John Chrysostom speaks; where the children, learning from the example of their elders, undertake a double apprenticeship, being opened to God and to their neighbour. How rich in meaning is the custom, in traditional Christian peasant societies, of always leaving a place free at the table, in case a stranger should knock; who might, for all they know, be the Stranger, God visiting his people under a familiar guise.

But surely the child is itself a little stranger who visits us. In however many reassuring ways it resembles us, it nevertheless remains radically different. As we know, we discover more and more as time goes by how much the child was wanted all along.

There is something magnificent in this freedom that can transform fertility from a biological urge into the desire for a vaster love. But it will happen only on one condition: however much the child was wanted, even if it had been possible to 'programme' it, it must have been welcomed in the beginning, and welcomed as a stranger.

Uncertainties

Nothing touches the mystery of personal existence like this theme of human love, which is why we should show reverence and restraint, and heed even more the evangelical caution against judging. We should remember the attitude of Jesus towards the woman 'taken in the very act of adultery' (John 8.3-11). We should remember the other, almost tangibly sensual account of the same Jesus allowing a prostitute to wipe his feet with her hair and anoint them with ointment and tears. The whole incident is suffused with eternity because of the imminence of death and transformation: 'She has done it to prepare me for burial' – already a spice-bearer. The Pharisee who receives Jesus says to himself, 'If this man were a prophet, he would have known who and what sort of woman this is who is touching him, for she is a sinner.' Jesus, perceiving his thoughts, says to him, 'Her sins, which are many, are forgiven, for she loved much; but he who is forgiven little, loves little.' And to the woman, 'Your faith has saved you; go in peace' (Luke 7.36-50, Matthew 26.6-13).

Finally we should remember the conversation with the Samaritan – a heretic! – at Jacob's well. Jesus quietly reminds her that she has had five husbands and that the man with whom she now lives is not even a husband. In so reminding her he is not judging, but his prescience must disclose to the woman who he is. 'Sir,' she says, 'I perceive that you are a prophet.' To this woman Jesus reveals not only the mystery of the living water, but also that 'God is spirit, and those who worship him must worship in spirit and truth' (John 4.1-42).

Talking to the woman taken in adultery, the sinner, the woman with five husbands, Jesus, in contrast to the Pharisees – and especially to Christian Pharisees – refuses to give too much importance to the tribulations of the flesh, or to make sex the scapegoat for our troubles; in these tribulations he sees only a sign of our common situation: 'Let him who is without sin among you be the first to throw a stone at her'. And he knows that humble people such as this woman with her disordered life will be the first to understand him.

That is why the Christian message, in such circumstances, is not a law that is imposed but something attractive that is proposed. It is not the business of the Church to dictate the laws on behalf of the State or to behave like some pressure group in obstructing them. The Church inspires and sanctifies, it does not compel; its business is to change hearts.

But more needs to be said. Even to her own children, the Church must be a merciful mother, not an impersonal juridical power. Her teachings about human love must be adapted, with immense care, to the circumstances of each person, by 'spiritual fathers' and bishops with the gift of discerning spirits. Among Eastern Christians this merciful adaptation, called 'economy', is actually a basic principle in the regular life of the Church. Orthodoxy is as insistent as Catholicism on the mystery of monogamy; more so indeed, since remarriage after the death of the spouse is not encouraged, and the rite has a penitential character. However, full weight is given to Christ's teaching that divorce is impossible to the Christian except in the case of *porneia* (i.e. where there has been adultery or fornication); where a couple has died because it is broken apart, the fact is recognized, and the divorced person can be married again. This sacrament is not like baptism, where the freedom of the person encounters constantly-offered grace. In marriage, grace is offered to a couple, i.e. to two human freedoms that are in agreement. In certain special cases, in the discernment of which the responsible ecclesiastical authorities must exercise the greatest care, it becomes apparent that common repentance and mutual forgiveness are no longer possible, that the couple no longer exists, and can no longer as such be a vehicle for the love which binds Christ and his Church. How can the Church debar these casualties of fate from communion? Would it dare to exclude from Christ the woman taken in adultery, the harlot, the woman with five husbands who now lives with a man who is not her husband? And are we any different, that we should cast the stone of the law?

Woman, the bearer of spices

After a long period of patriarchy, women today wish to be treated as human beings in their own right, free and responsible individuals. The leaven of the Gospel is at work, setting us free at last from the old pagan structures. But because the necessary fight for social equality has so often had to be waged against men, there is now some uncertainty about woman's true identity, what it means to be feminine. The body, the soul, motherhood – these are certainly symbols, but because of the way they have so often been interpreted, they have become more than ever tokens of women's inferiority. In Christian thought, masculine and feminine do not form a hierarchy, but are modes of the one human nature. As we have said, both are present in each man and woman, so that the woman, when she asserts her dignity as a person *against* the man, comes to resemble him, exaggerating, in her hatred, her own masculinity to the detriment of her femininity. Hence the ambiguity of the modern Western 'women's liberation' movement. Women here are rightly rebellious against a diffused Freudianism which, unwittingly reviving old Aristotelian and scholastic prejudices, sees the movement as a sort of male failure. Women are protesting against a hedonistic society which turns them into erotic objects and uses their nakedness as a means of publicity – bringing into being a vast brothel of the imagination. They desire real partnership

with men, and a full share in city life, where they proved themselves a long time ago; their energetic, assertive sympathy awakens
them to the plight of the downtrodden everywhere – in the third
world or the shanty towns, in despised minorities, in the factories
where breadwinning is still likely to entail the loss of the soul.
However, since a truly spiritual understanding is wanting, chaos
looms, and the relationship of domination, instead of giving place
to creative tension, is reversed. Violence creates a type of homo-
sexual Amazonian dominatrix; ignorance of the disciplines of
transformation, once the old dams have burst, releases nothing
but the instincts and primitive magic.

It is therefore important, in this area as well, to develop and
quietly insist upon a truly Christian way of thinking. We might
suggest, like Paul Evdokimov, that the masculine side of human
nature particularly reflects the Word, which organizes and defines,
and the feminine the Holy Spirit, which inspires, consoles and
incarnates. As we said before, the Semitic word for Spirit, *Ruach*,
is often feminine. Moreover in the language of the Church there is
a strict correlation between the Spirit of all holiness – *Panagion* –
and the woman par excellence, the Mother of God, venerated as
the 'all holy' – *Panagia*. In an early Christian text, the *Didascalia
Apostolorum*, we read, on the subject of the diaconate, which was
then conferred on women as well as men, 'The deacon has the place
of Christ, and you will love him. You will honour the deaconesses
in the place of the Holy Spirit'.

These remarks enable us to understand the symbolic nature of
the characteristics of the male and female.

Masculine movement, whether sexual or in mere walking, intellectual activity as well as physical, is at once linear and jerky; while
feminine movement suggests irradiation and continuity. There is a
similar contrast between the angular geometry of the man's body
and the harmonious continuity of the woman's.

The man, like an archer, goes straight for the mark. His will is
tensed to surmount the obstacle. The woman responds by an act

of presence in which the abstract will is less important than the resonance of her whole being. Expressiveness matters more to her than accomplishment. A little boy overacts, his sister dresses up.

The man explodes – into laughter or anger; the woman flows like water, and like water she can smile.

The man is the conqueror, ranging afar; his aim is distant, his utterance is poetical. The woman attends to the present moment, she brings us back to material things, she is ironical.

The man makes his escape, the woman yields. Worry belongs to her, and often devotedness.

The man thinks with his head, the woman with her whole being. She carries the child in her flesh, she is in collusion with life.

But to progress from this ambiguous description to the truth of the feminine and masculine as the divine image requires spiritual training and an understanding of transfiguration.

In Eastern churches, above the 'royal doors' which stand before the altar and in front of which the faithful receive communion, there are usually portrayed, in an attitude of prayer on either side of Christ in majesty, the Mother of God and St John Baptist. Evdokimov sees in these two figures the true nature of the masculine and the feminine displayed. The Baptist, in the tradition of Elijah, internalizes his natural violence to 'prepare the way of the Lord', in the certainty that 'he must increase, but I must decrease'. Here man the wide-ranging conqueror discovers his cross and his transformation. The spiritual man, according to the image of the Baptist, is not the bridegroom who dominates and possesses, but the friend of the heavenly bridegroom, the one who knows that the woman, as much as anybody, is close to God. As for the Mother of God, 'she gives birth to the divine form on earth and the human form in heaven', fulfilling her spiritual motherhood. In her image, the child-bearing by which the woman is saved, to quote St Paul, is not biological predestination, nor simply the maternal instinct, which as we know can be possessive to the point of suffocation. In this image true motherhood is transfigured in the one who, at the foot of the cross, received the great commandment to be the Mother of all. Pointing to his beloved disciple, the crucified Lord said, 'Woman, behold, your son'. And who among us is not beloved? Only this sacrificial motherhood, which is disinterested, and perfectly compatible with celibacy, can bring out the meaning of physiological motherhood. Ultimately, as Evdokimov says, the spiritual vocation of the woman is to 'bring God to birth in ravaged souls'.

Every human being, man or woman, according to his or her nature, is called to a degree of virility – remember the strong women of the Bible – and also, in relation to God, a degree of femininity. Progress in the spiritual life leads men as well as women to a quasi-feminine attitude in the presence of the mystery. That is why the incarnation was accomplished through a woman, who is now at the heart of the communion of saints. But when the man and the woman, enriched by God, turn to face the world, each rediscovers, transfigured, that aspect of human nature which is predominant in him or her: the one is an arouser, a combatant, the other 'covers life with her maternal protection'. The man hurts in order to arouse, the woman heals and cures; according to Fedorov, 'Every woman is a spice-bearer'. So there are two attitudes basic to the Christian spiritual life: vigilance, which is manly, and tenderness, which is feminine.

Beginning with Adam, humanity proceeds by way of the last Adam – Christ, human and divine – to fulfilment in a woman: the Mother of God. The Church is, in Christ, the Church of the Holy Spirit; it is based not on hierarchy but on holiness. The priesthood is ordained to serve this central principle, not to convey any essential superiority to its bearers. It is reserved to men because the priest, as celebrant, is the image of Christ, and Christ, while undoubtedly possessing human nature in its fullness, is a man, and not a woman or a hermaphrodite. But Christ came only in order that the Spirit might descend, and that there might appear, beneath the tongues of fire at Pentecost, a renewed humanity, at whose heart there is a woman.

The demand of women for priestly orders is evidence of a forgetting of the Spirit and of God's transforming power. It is the bitter fruit of the clericalization of the Church.

We must rediscover the ministry of deaconesses, which expresses the spiritual motherhood mysteriously bound to the Spirit.

And it ought to be possible for a woman to be a priest's wife, and exercise in her own way, which is not functional but personal, the priesthood of discretion and dedication in the Spirit.

We can now see that man and woman are complementary, not by exercising separate functions, but because their personal existence together makes up a mysterious whole.

No longer is *Eros* the impersonal fascination of the flesh, or the Platonic or Tantric use of the other person as a means to ecstasy; it is the looking to another person for a communion of soul and body. In the difficult dialogue of true love, so difficult because to refine and deepen it takes a lifetime of faithful marriage, in this dialogue where 'the soul is the form of the body' there are two persons recognizing each other little by little. For the man, the woman is no longer woman in general, the universal female or 'the eternal feminine', she is that *thou* which the other aspect of her humanity helps him to call by name. And similarly for her with the man. All subordination is reciprocal, a giving of freedom to the other person. Each transcends the desire to possess which encloses him/her in solitude and death. The human being, no longer domineering or an object of scorn, but living in communion, appears twofold and one, in a mutual exchange of honour, celebration and tenderness.

'We carry this treasure in earthen vessels.' But our long journeyings through the night will never efface the memory of that first glimmer of dawn, that paschal fire of true love.

6

God and Caesar

The kingdom of God and the kingdom of Caesar

'From now on politics will be our religion'; so wrote Feuerbach, a little before Marx socialized God. And looking now at the emptiness created by industrial civilization, we can see how right he was. With the headlong progress of technology and the development of global civilization, there is a greater need than ever for a sense of purpose, the influence of the Spirit, a new marriage covenant between the human race and the earth. Our society seems to have no aim beyond unlimited economic growth. The Spirit is not spectacular, so the image-machines offer us 'idols' and 'passions', the slick presentation masking the absurdity of it all. The spiritual under-development of some combines with the material under-development of others to create the 'third world' in our shanty-towns.

So the rebellion on the part of many young people expresses two cravings which are complementary: the craving of some for meaning, and that of others for dignity. We hear a great deal about 'changing your life', and this happened in the demonstrations when those old enemies, the red flag and the black flag, at last joined forces, blindly foreshadowing, in their assertion of the unity of all and the uniqueness of each, the communion of the Trinity. The now-mythical revolution was the misdirected expression of a much deeper need. Do not misunderstand the saying, 'everything is politics'; the key word is *everything*, and politics is the opium, if not of the people, at least of a younger generation and an intelligentsia who, in denying God, are seeking him.

It is therefore time for Christians to remember that the infra-structure of history is nothing other than the relationship between humanity and the living God. In history the human and divine are blended, the emphasis being sometimes on God, to the exclusion of humanity, and sometimes on humanity, to the exclusion of God. The meaning, the centre of history is in Christ, truly God and truly human, and consequently 'maximum human'; its creative impulse is in the Spirit and our freedom.

The human race is not only the child of the earth and of history. It is also the image of God, called to become the adopted child of God, bearer of the Spirit, 'god by grace'. The Cross has mortally wounded the pagan religions of the earth and the totalitarian regimes of history. The tension between the Kingdom of God and the kingdom of Caesar is irreducible until the final transfiguration (which will bring with it the final overthrow of the devil); it points to that transfiguration and hastens its approach, opening the space of the Spirit in which the person, also irreducible, has room to move. And if Christendom has disappeared, it is certainly because it failed to recognize this tension and denied personal freedom. History, from the empty tomb onwards, cannot be closed in on itself; it is pervaded by the expectation of the Kingdom, where the earth and the suffering of humankind will be transfigured through the free communion of persons united to God.

That is why the early Christians refused to testify to the divinity of Caesar and asserted that Christ alone is divine, that only by life in him can human beings share in divinity. When there was no other way, they kept history open by martyrdom; the act by which the Christian, in the face of overweening power, enters utterly into the passion and resurrection of the Lord, consecrating earth and history with his blood, transforming them, despite everything, into offerings. The first Christians prayed for Caesar – even when Caesar's name was Nero – and at the same time humbly asked him to tolerate their existence which would be, was already, a blessing to the Empire.

Whenever Caesar, as an individual or an institution, pretends to explain humankind entirely by history, he is demanding to be worshipped.

The last of the righteous

The first task of the Church and of Christians is therefore to open up history to the eternity whither she is destined to 'pass' one day in a final Passover, whither she is already 'passing' by the prayers and the blessing of the liturgy and of liturgical people. To those who see with the 'eye of the heart', the reintegrating power of the sacraments holds the world in being, preserves history from decay and slowly permeates the life of the universe with eternity. The prayer and love of the poor, of the innocent, of the 'fools for Christ' multiply the effect of this eucharistic blessing, and make a way for the divine energies to penetrate the world and act upon it; these radiate from personal Love, and it is only personal freedom that can open history to them, just as only the fiat of the Mother of God made possible the incarnation of the Word. That is why the secret masters of history, although they do not know it, are people of adoration.

The Church has always taught that Christians, by their *active presence* and their intercession, safeguard cosmic order and human society, and raise them to the status of offerings. The most ancient 'apology' for Christianity that we know, that of Aristides, composed at the time of the first persecutions, plainly states, 'Of this there is no doubt, that it is because of the intercession of Christians that the world continues to exist' (XVI.6). This notion has its roots in the Old Testament, where Abraham, by prodigious bargaining, secured the preservation of Sodom, provided there should be found in it only ten righteous men. Christians are called to supply the righteous who were lacking in Sodom. Thus, in the Acts of the Apostles (27.33-44), we see St Paul, on his way to Rome under guard, rescuing his fellow passengers from despair and death when their ship was wrecked. And he did it in an almost eucharistic way: when all seemed lost, 'he took bread, and giving thanks to God in the presence of all he broke it and began to eat'; then they all regained hope, and received from the food the strength they needed for swimming to land or clinging to the wreckage.

Not only Christianity but the other Semitic religions, Islam and Judaism, recognize this function of the 'last of the righteous'. The Talmud says that the world is kept in existence by the intercession of thirty six righteous who are renewed from generation to generation and 'receive the Presence daily'. In Christianity, from the 4th century onwards, this ministry of intercession tended to be concentrated in the prayer of the monks. An Egyptian bishop of the time wrote to the hermits: 'The universe is saved by your prayers; thanks to your supplications, the rain descends on the earth, the earth is covered in green, the trees are laden with fruit' (Serapion of Thmuis, *Letter to the Monks*, 3;PG,XL,928 D-929 A).

Intercession, the Church's benediction, is an invisible pillar joining heaven to earth, which enables nature and history to bear fruit, and this pillar is the work of the saints. Those who are alive today go unrecognized. In appearance they may be unremarkable or alarming, but they are in the presence of the Risen Lord, united to him. On the beach you find shells disfigured by accretions of sand, seaweed, and marine worms. But when you turn them over, the purest mother-of-pearl appears, iridescent with the sky and resonant with the sea. So it is with the Church. When the Lamb breaks the seals of the book of the true history, we shall find that all the fruits of history have resulted from the unacknowledged reign of the saints. We shall discover that battles have been less important than the cry of the angry and distressed calling upon God, the plea of Job and so many like him, and the publican's prayer of faith...

In the present crisis, which is a crisis of meaning, we must learn to see the Church once again as essentially the mystery of sanctification, abounding in paschal joy and the peace 'which the world cannot give', which 'passes all understanding'. It is the chief task of the Church to nourish us with that peace and joy, renewing the Church in the parishes, making them real eucharistic communities where people can learn to live in communion. In places like this we could take refuge from a life which is both frenzied and solitary, where all we are offered in compensation is anarchy and the chance to lose ourselves in instant sex or political extremism. Coming to these places without any ulterior motive, we could at last find beauty and tenderness, and the knowledge that death has been overcome, that there is no more need for scapegoats; being united in adoration, we could talk to each other freely.

The first Christian communities were each called an *agape*, divinely inspired love, and the word more specifically denoted the meal of fellowship which followed, or surrounded, the eucharist. The Church urgently needs to restore these occasions of sharing and mutual help, *around the eucharist* (otherwise the common meal would remain mortal food) where the presence of the sacrament makes our service of one another sacramental also, and our need of celebration is purified and fulfilled. On the mount of transfiguration Peter said, 'It is good for us to be here'. If you have taken part in the paschal vigil in an Orthodox church, when we all embrace each other while proclaiming the truth of the resurrection, you will know what I mean. With the proliferation of these parishes, perhaps linked to monastic communities who understand how to balance withdrawal from society and engagement with it, there would be no need to work out how to change the world; it would inevitably change of its own accord.

The Romanesque and Byzantine civilizations, Chartres and Hagia Sophia, were born of the blood of the martyrs and the prayers of the monks. The saints of the Merovingian age, who are now almost forgotten, laid the invisible foundations of France. Francis of Assisi, made possible the first Italian renaissance, when earthly creatures were seen in the light of God's joy; and the prayers of Athos, like the work of Dostoevsky five centuries later, fertilized the art of Mistra and Kariye Camii. Little did the future St Sergius know, as he went deep into the forest intent on his 'work of silence', that he carried within himself the victory of Kulikovo and the Trinity of Rublev. And who can tell the secret connection between the Russian martyrs, between the wars and the wise compassion, the 'sorrowful joy' of Pasternak's *Doctor Zhivago* or the work of Solzhenitsyn, which is the decisive cure for Western nihilism? Perhaps the prayers of the early Church and the Middle Ages stored up the energy which later sustained modern humanism; but the supply has now run out, so we must drill for more...

Only people who are drunk with God, who wish history to be swallowed up in eternity, can make civilization fruitful. History is renewed by those who transcend it: 'Thy kingdom come!'

The sacrament of our neighbour

The essence of God the Trinity is love, so personal existence directed towards God can only be existence in communion. 'By this it may be seen who are the children of God, and who are the children of the devil: whoever does not do right is not of God, nor he who does not love his brother' (1 John 3.10). In St Matthew's overpowering portrayal of the Judgement, Christ says to those who are truly righteous: 'I was hungry and you gave me food, I was thirsty and you gave me drink, I was a stranger and you welcomed me, I was naked and you clothed me...' And when the righteous are astonished, the Son of Man lets them into the great secret: *'Truly, I say to you, as you did it to one of the least of these my brethren, you did it to me'* (Matthew 25.34-40). St John Chrysostom, commenting on this text with his usual realism, has spoken of the 'sacrament of the brother', above all of the 'least' of the brethren, the poor. This great Patriarch of Constantinople, who defended spiritual liberty and the rights of the poor against oppression, even to the extent of martyrdom, stated emphatically that the poor person is *another*

Christ and the sacrament of the eucharist must be continued by working for greater justice, an 'alms' which is concerned not with feelings of pity but with fair shares, or even with better town planning. In the first Church at Jerusalem, the mother and the pattern of all the Churches, all things were had in common, and for Christians, throughout their rich history, this has remained the outstanding image, not of perfect economics which would resolve all difficulties, but of the triumph of the will over selfishness and meanness, so that all might be of one heart and mind. Several of the Fathers, such as Basil of Caesarea and John Chrysostom in the East, or Ambrose of Milan in the West, taught not only in word but in action that private property is relative in character. They fiercely disputed the right to inherit the means of production, and demonstrated that natural riches belong only to God and must be used for the good of all. At the same time, after the example of Paul who made tents, they restored the dignity of work, which was considered servile in the ancient world, but which for them was the exercise of human responsibility for the universe and the basis of a common life in which communion could grow. In the conformism of the Constantinian period, when the Church membership was inflated with conventional believers, the parishes partly lost the power of *agape* and the common life. This necessitated a 'sanctified rebellion' in the form of monasteries, communities founded on apostolic love, where the witness of the first church at Jerusalem might be continued in a new historical setting. The monasteries being generally open to the public, people could see that all the monks worked with their hands, as has always been the custom in the East, and learn that self-sacrifice demands also the sacrifice of riches. And when, thanks, among other things, to their vast land clearances, they had great riches to dispose of, they used them in the true service of society, which was combined, in 'barbaric' regions, with a strong cultural influence.

We know now that the widespread following of holy poverty which shook Christendom in the Middle Ages and in early modern times owed much to the teaching of Chrysostom. These movements, and their cruel repression, mark one of the most ruinous schisms in the history of Christianity: *the schism between the sacrament of the altar and the sacrament of the brother*. The Church preserved the mystery and the mysticism of the Risen Lord, but in such a distorted fashion – as we see in the degeneration of monastic life and the growth of an individualistic pietism ill-adapted to creative ethics – that Christians tended to forget the crucified Christ of history, especially when the history was that of the industrial revolution. These distortions are clearly illustrated in the evolution of the diaconate; in the early Church, it was the deacon who extended the eucharist into service of the community; in his person, representing the bishop, social service became sacramental. But today, the diaconal ministry has effectively disappeared in the West, despite a half-hearted attempt to revive it, and in the East has become purely liturgical.

Cut adrift from the eucharist, which alone could give it life, however little, the sacrament of the brother was diverted into a desire, hopeful or violent, for Utopia, or an ardent millenarianist longing for the final catastrophe which will usher in the reign of the saints. This brings us to the beginning of modern socialism, which is a combination of evangelical fervour, humanism that has become atheistical and the resentment born of powerlessness.

We now feel that the time is clearly approaching for this schism to be healed. We must put an end to the common Christian schizophrenia whereby, on Sunday, we are caught up into heaven (in the East) or filled with good intentions (in the West) only to sink back during the week into the business of this world. It is not a matter of replacing the sacrament of the altar with that of the brother, as 'progressive' people do, which would mean leaving history to its own devices, admitting it to be, after all, no more than a dance of death; but rather of giving full weight to the ethical aspect of the eucharist. Now since the beginning of the century, especially from Péguy and Berdyaev onwards, the spirit of prophecy has been awake in Christianity; the sap, rising little by little through countless lives humbly devoted to the daily struggle of the Beatitudes, has at last found two supremely worthy spokesmen, John XXIII and Athenagoras I. In Eastern Europe, Orthodoxy, despite its tendency to servility, has refused to appoint itself the guardian of private property; there the bravest call for religious freedom and the 'disestablishment' of Marxism, while affirming that Christianity is compatible with a non-totalitarian socialism.

For the rest, this is not a question of 'socialism' or of the latest magic formula for universal happiness. It is a matter of allowing the Gospel full freedom to take effect in society at large.

And that is the only formula: active, resourceful, dogged love, with no illusion that total and lasting success is to be had in history – that would be a strange misjudgement of the depth of evil – but inspired by a vision of whole humanity, or rather, of divine-humanity.

Hope and freedom

As Christians we know that by participating in history we are not going to turn it into the Kingdom of God. But our horizon is not limited to history; we know that Christ is coming again in glory to raise all the dead and, through them, the flesh of the world and all that history has created. With this hope we have no need of Utopia.

Christians are making ready within history a transformation which will surpass it, the transformation that is already secretly accomplished in Christ. Thus they escape the dilemma of 'all or nothing'; nor do they simply accept things as they are, like the hopeless or the well-to-do. They are watchful for every opportunity of promoting freedom, justice, or dignity. Their struggle – an inner one to begin with – is neither conservative nor revolutionary, nor even both at once. The conservativism of Christians is not the same as the cynicism and fear felt by those who have too much, who are all the more willing to theorize about the intractability of history for having themselves benefited from it. Christians cannot stay far from the abandoned and the rebellious. But even while aware of the chances of life, and their tragic consequences in history, we nevertheless know that there are principles, virtually biological laws, by which social life is harmonized with the life of the universe; that the tension between the individual and society is irreducible, and that in politics more than anywhere else 'he who would be an angel behaves like a beast'; the makers of paradise have been tormentors from hell, and the liver of Prometheus is gnawed away by pollution. Humankind needs justice and happiness, but also risk, transcendence, the profound tragedy of existence. The struggle against the 'spirit of heaviness', against stupidity and hatred, is never-ending. Only a hope anchored beyond the world – but already transforming the world through personal beings – can give us the patience to serve life without falling into bitterness or despair.

Christians may not be revolutionary as popular mythology understands the term, but they know that there is a revolutionary force within Christianity, that of Christ the vanquisher of death. This force can alter the makeup of the person. And if this change takes place simultaneously in several people who are in communion, then the world begins to change, and a civilization is founded.

The desire of modern society to forget death is blindingly obvious; people are set free from basic ills but abandoned without mercy to finiteness, a 'dead life'. This is undoubtedly the pathetic truth about a civilization based on happiness, and it is why people revolt against it. Marxism socializes absolute value, evading personal death – the only real kind – in favour of the prolongation, and the supposed upward progress, of the species. Fascism, in its earliest form, was a glorification of death in battle.

By faith in Christ the vanquisher of death, by our foretaste of the resurrection, and by the hope of the Kingdom, we ought to be able to cure the fundamental dread within and around us, and so set people free to live their lives to the full. To make something of our lives in the transitory cities of this world, we must hold together the recollection of death and of God. Being mindful of the passing of all things, and also of the 'passover' of all things in God, we are cured of idolatry and nihilism; we relativize in order to eternize.

The other dimension of witness in the city can only be freedom. The Churches should repent bitterly for having relied for so many centuries on the sword of the State. Today, to the astonishment of young people in Eastern Europe, Christianity appears essentially as the revelation of the person and of freedom. That is why Christians, engaged in history, must make freedom not only the end but the means. According to Chigalev, Dostoevsky's genial *gnostic of history* in *The Devils*, unlimited freedom comes about when 'those who know' have unlimited power. It is for us to preserve personal freedom from both social and ideological enslavement. It is for us to bear witness that God is the space of freedom, and that if humanity is not in God's image it will always be in bondage to nature and history. Now respecting the image of God in people means above all not imposing good on them. People need to be shown, especially by the attraction of communion, that true freedom – the freedom that enables us to transcend ourselves in love – requires a long schooling in death-and-resurrection; otherwise the only freedom will be chaos inhabited by wild beasts. The 'divine marquis' showed clearly, at the heart of the French Revolution, that if we abandon ourselves to 'nature', fraternity turns into the brotherhood of Cain. But the only creative constraints are those that are self-imposed. 'A young man came to a holy monk seeking to be instructed in the way of fullness. The old man breathed not a word. The other asked why he was silent. 'Am I your superior that I should command you?' he replied. 'I will say nothing; but, if you like, do what you see me do."

Our cities desperately need the presence of Christians, enlivened by hope and intent on freedom; when they have studied the workings of society, like everyone else, they must make it their sole task to permeate its density with an unquenchable desire for communion. Fedorov said, 'Our social programme is the Trinity;

everything else is society in decay.' In this enterprise there can be no conflict between the insistence on fair dealing, the setting up of model communities and the reform of society; the last after all simply means that we house, clothe and feed, as we are bound to do, the 'thou' who is our neighbour, all over the world. When St John Chrysostom began to preach the 'sacrament of the brother', he conceived the idea of reorganizing the society of Antioch in such a way that poverty would be abolished. But society is an aspect of the person, not the other way round, and however ethical the social institutions are, they are of no value unless they are created by and for persons. Society and morality are bound together, and morality is purified and elevated only by a schooling in contemplation, disciplined prayer and practical love. This happens only over a long period and within a gradually developing common tradition. If we are all to know what it is to be noble, then nobility needs to be embodied in monks and knights. Eventually the tradition is exhausted, and life must be fertilized anew by eternity.

The love of enemies

The theologians of violence forget the Beatitudes. The theologians of non-violence forget that history consists of tragedies. But amongst the violence of history, it is the duty of Christians to manifest the love of enemies, which is the strength of Christ himself. The love of enemies, exercised in the most extreme circumstances, is the only cure for our political neurosis, the desire to escape one's own death while projecting it on to the enemy; and the cure begins with me. Only thus shall we achieve a life that is creative and free. But to erect non-violence into a system is to dream of recreating the Constantinian period in a sublimated form. The 'peacemakers' are to be called 'children of God', but we must not forget that the Son of God was crucified. Nothing is more confusing than the turning of spiritual disciplines, like fasting, intended to render the world secretly permeable to the divine light, into means of psychological restraint on society. The life of Gandhi was so fruitful precisely because of his constant willingness to lay it down, and the same was true of Martin Luther King. The belief was common in the Middle Ages that it was the duty of a Christian king to die a martyr's death for the sake of his friends – and his enemies; Saint-Just's bitter remark that nobody can reign with impunity was answered before he made it.

It is the Church's business not to impose methods, even non-violent ones, but to witness in season and out of season to the creative power of love. The problem is not one of violence or non-violence at all; and the solution, which can never be more than partial, lies in the ability to transform, as far as possible and in every circumstance of history, destructive violence into creative power. The cross which, as Berdyaev memorably said, causes the rose of worldly existence to bloom afresh, here signifies not resignation, but service; not weakness, but creative activity.

The king and his fool

At the heart of Christianity is the tendency to desacralize power in order to sanctify it through the person who exercises it. When he was tempted in the wilderness, Jesus decisively rejected the worship always demanded by the prince, and the princes, of this world; but he asked his followers to render to Caesar the things that belong to him and reminded Pilate that he would have no power at all over the Son of Man if that power had not been given him from above. In the same way, as we have said, the early Church, while denouncing the divinized State as the Beast of the Apocalypse, prayed for the authorities.

Later, with the arrival of Christendom, the Church conferred unction on the Christian King, cherishing him as a bearer of a special gift of the Spirit, almost equivalent to crucifixion, the gift of kingship. In the East, chiefly, but also in the West during the long struggle against the theocratic claims of the Papacy, the best relationship between Church and State was found to be that of 'symphony', or mutual agreement, in which the ecclesiastical hierarchy did not pretend to possess the source of political power. The king, as the representative of the laity and of its 'royal priesthood', bore the image of Christ in a special way. In him power was sanctified by becoming creative service, the restriction of evil, the establishment in the midst of chaos of an enclave of order and peace.

There was a certain grandeur about this endeavour. Combining in creative tension with the monks' longing for eternity here and now, it encouraged the ennobling of daily life by true beauty. The king and his people received communion in the church; but they also met together on holidays in the square outside.

The experiment failed because it did not respect freedom.

Today it is the duty of each Christian to assume the 'royal priesthood', by which power is sanctified through service and creativity. Indeed, it is vitally important that we recognize the genuinely religious significance of creative activity. We shall defeat the clericalism of the Church and the clericalism of ideology – both exercised by the same type of castrati – only if, in every field, we nourish the vocation to be truly royal, to transform violence into creative energy, to increase life and beauty: in short, to be good gardeners, who prune not haphazardly but to make the tree bear fruit. And, certainly, to be crucified between violence and creation, is the inescapable 'passion' of kings.

A king, therefore, finds personal peace not in monastic seclusion but in creative tension. King-priest, because he tries to symbolize the eternal in the flesh of earthly cities. King-prophet, because in the face of all the idols he proclaims the true Kingdom.

The king, moreover, never comes without his fool. The world of the Beatitudes is a looking-glass world in which the ponderousness and pompousness of our own side are pricked and burst. And we are kings of an invisible Kingdom. The royalty of the Christian is inseparable from a certain buffoonery towards all over-serious or possessive behaviour. One of the highest forms of sanctity is seen in 'fools for Christ', those 'innocents' sometimes found in the rougher parts of town living among people whom the Pharisees despise as immoral. While seeming to clown, they can suddenly strip away the dead layers from the soul, leaving it bare, bringing it face to face with death, or love.

These strange vocations flourish on the edges of big cities. And every village has its idiot, who knows its secrets.

These are the voices to which the king listens when he listens to his fool.

The fool prevents the monk and the king from glorying, the one in his unworldly detachment and the other in his worldly importance. He reminds the one that he is much less advanced spiritually than the cobbler who prays that all might be saved, or the bandit whose heart was one day pierced with pity, or the mother burdened with family cares who never gives up hope. To the other he says, *Memento mori.*

Today we must all, in dealing with the world, exercise and internalize the two functions which, when society was Christian, constituted the two pillars of the people of God: that of the monk and that of the king. But let us not forget to be our own fool as well.

Towards a creative secularism

In the inescapably pluralist life of the city today, Christians must strive for a creative secularism. An open civilization, free from ideocracy, must not be a spiritual desert abandoned to the instincts by the blind forces of production. Kirkegaard thought it necessary 'to go more deeply into man as he actually exists' before daring to speak to him of God. More than a thousand years before, the hardiest of ascetics, St John Climacus, remarked that true beauty is never profane: 'When we hear singing,' he said, 'let us be moved with love towards God; for those who love God are touched with a holy joy, a divine emotion and a tenderness which brings them to tears when they listen to beautiful harmony, *whether the songs are profane or spiritual'* (*The Ladder,* 15th step).

We must hope to attract the post-industrial society of today by a rich, complex, open anthropology, which by its very openness respects the 'fathomlessness' of the person and is capable of growing into a 'theo-anthropology'. Everyone now realizes that human beings need not only bread but friendship and beauty, not only abundance but restraint, not only the power of machines but a renewed respect for God's creation, not only education of the mind but a greater capacity for celebration. The rampant techno-logical revolution will be mastered only if we can incorporate in it the non-technical values and dimensions of humanity. The gen-eration gap will disappear when we no longer walk backwards towards death, but receive wisdom and pass it on. The martial instinct, formerly having no outlet but destruction and adventuring, will lose its power to corrupt when it is incorporated into disci-pline: individual discipline in spirituality and art, and collective discipline in the great 'wars of life' that humanity must wage to cure the wounds of the third world, to curb the excesses of technology, and to re-establish harmony with the universe.

So Christian witness today must be directed towards the divine-humanism that urban society needs. A religion that set God against humanity and failed to recognize the 'royal' character of creativity (since it comes from the Holy Spirit) fell victim to the purifying zeal of the great reductionists and the huge advances in our understanding of human nature. But today people who are cut off from the Holy Spirit are in danger of death. Modern humanism needs to be openly acknowledged as belonging within divine-humanism, thus revealing Marx, Nietzche and Freud to be *also* forerunners of this movement. And at the heart of the human race as it grows into unity, there is the vision of a Church undivided once more, combining the ethical and cultural energy of the Western Church with the unshakeable faith of Orthodoxy, which in turn forms a bridge to the most distant Oriental Churches. This transformed Church would make no demands, impose no burdens. It would be a source of meaning, freedom and creative love. It would promote the unity in diversity, already realized within itself, of persons, peoples, races, and cultures, in the image of the Communion of the Trinity. It would reveal the full significance of science and technology, setting them in the context of the Resurrection. The Patriarch Athenagoras speaking in 1969 to an Italian journalist said, 'The world now stands at a moment when all values are being put to the test. Scientific discoveries and advancing technology, space travel, rapid social change, spiritual upheaval, the conflict between the generations ... create a confusion never known before. And in this confusion we are often tempted to lose heart. But we must not give in to this temptation, even for an instant, or abandon ourselves to despair. The state of the world is that of childbirth, and childbirth is always accompanied by hope. We contemplate the present situation with immense Christian hope and a deep awareness of our responsibility for the kind of world which will emerge from this childbirth. And there lies the Church's opportunity: united, it must provide a Christian direction to the new world which is being born' (*Avvenire*, 12 January 1969).

7

Human Beings and the Cosmos

The mystery of created being

For the Christian the world is not an orphan; nor is it simply an emanation of the absolute. Springing fresh from the hands of the living God, there it stands, desired by God, rejoicing and delighting in him with the joy described in the psalms and in the book of Job, when the morning stars sang together – a 'musical commandment', a 'marvellously composed hymn', as St Gregory of Nyssa said in his commentary on the Psalms (PG,XLIV,441 B).

The creature is a ceaseless movement from nothingness to existence, attracted by the infinite; a movement during which time, space, and material form are simultaneously bestowed. 'This world is a semi-being in perpetual flux, constantly evolving, never still; and beyond, the attentive ear is attuned to another reality' (Paul Florensky).

So the Christian views nature as a new reality, true and dynamic, quickened, as the Fathers say, by a 'luminous' force put in it by God to draw it towards transcendence. Consequently, according to Florensky, only in Christianity can the true meaning of createdness be seen, where all scientific research into nature rests on the biblical revelation: 'Only then could something created be seen as more than the devil's bauble, a sort of emanation, or illusion of divinity, like the rainbow in a drop of water; only then could the world be thought of as a creature of God, autonomous in his being, his righteousness and his authority.'

At the same time, the glory of God is revealed at the very root of things, for the roots of the creature are essentially heavenly. According to its *logos*, its 'name', the living word by which and in which God holds it in being, the creature expresses the divine glory after its own fashion and by its very existence. For 'there is one glory of the sun, and another glory of the moon, and another glory of the stars; for star differs from star in glory' (1 Cor. 15.41).

Where these complementary approaches meet, the Christian idea of the symbol is born. The world is not God, but his temple, his 'place', as the contemplatives call the 'heart'. The more plentiful nature is, the more alive and bursting with its own vital energy, the greater is its symbolic significance. The symbol is not a 'veneer' applied to things; it is their very substance, the dynamism of their nature called to fulfil itself in God.

Humanity, priest and king of the universe

The universe is present to Man as the first revelation he receives, and it is his task to interpret it creatively, to give conscious utterance to the ontological praise of things. The world is also, in impersonally female guise, presented to Man, to be united with him in a mystical marriage, forming one flesh with him. The whole sensible universe is an extension of our body. Or rather, as we have already said, and in biblical terms, our body is simply the form which the person, our 'living soul', impresses on the universal 'dust'. There is no discontinuity between the flesh of the world and that of Man; the world is the body of humanity. Man is a 'little world', a 'microcosm', which sums up, distils, recapitulates the degrees of created being, so he knows the world from the inside. The first account of creation in Genesis (1.26-31) describes Man the microcosm as being created *after* the other beings, but assimilated to them by the same blessing, appearing as the summit and completion of evolution.

All the same, the human being is, as we know, much more than a microcosm; the human being is a person in the image of God. In our personal freedom we transcend the universe, not in order to abandon it but to contain it, to utter its meaning, to mediate grace to it. Through humanity, the universe is called to become the 'image of the image' (St Gregory of Nyssa). It is in this sense that the Fathers understand the second account of the creation (Genesis 2.4-25) which sees in Man the basic principle of the created world. Only Man is quickened by the very breath of God, and without him the 'plants' could not grow, as if they were rooted in him. And it is he who 'names' the animals, discerning their spiritual essences. Only Man – who is priest as well as king – can bring out the secret sacramentality of the universe. Adam was put in the world to 'cultivate' it, to perfect its beauty. It was Vladimir Soloviev's profound observation that the vocation of the human race is to become a collective cosmic Messiah and 'subdue the earth', that is to say transfigure it.

For the universe, therefore, humanity is its hope of obtaining grace and being united to God. Man is also its risk of failure and degeneration, because, if he turns away from God, he will see only the outward appearance of things and impose a false 'name' on them. St Paul, in a basic text, describes a state of fallenness and redemption, but one where we see revived, in Christ, the vocation of humanity as mediator: 'The creation waits with eager longing for the revealing of [men as] the sons of God; for the creation was subjected to futility, not of its own will, but by the will of him [man, the mediator] who subjected it in hope; because the creation itself will be set free from its bondage to decay and obtain the glorious liberty of the children of God' (Romans 8.19-21). So everything that happens in humanity is of universal significance, being imprinted on the universe. Humanity's fate determines the fate of the cosmos. The biblical revelation, understood symbolically, confronts us with an uncompromising anthropocentrism, which is not physical but spiritual. Because Man is at once 'microcosm and *microtheos*', both a summing up of the universe and the image of God; and because God, in order to unite himself to the world, finally became a human being; humanity is the spiritual axis of all creation, at every level, in every sphere. The saints see the universe in God, pervaded by his energies, held whole and entire, but tiny, in his hand. The movement of modern science from geocentrism to heliocentrism, and thence to the complete absence of centre in physical infinity, poses no threat to the pivotal character of humankind in God, but gives it a renewed significance. There is nowhere that the unlimited universe can be situated but in the creative love of God in which the human race can consciously share. The indefiniteness of the world is consequently situated in sanctified humanity and becomes the symbol of the 'deep calling to deep'. Certainly, as Nietzsche declared while he was announcing the death of God, for those who reject or know nothing of the Living God, there is neither height nor depth, but only cold and shadows. But for those who believe and know – and this is the joy to which all are called – the heart of the saints is the 'place of God' and therefore the centre of the world; better than that, the heart contains the world and so situates it in love.

Certain Greek fathers, like Gregory of Nyssa, and certain Russian theologians in the first half of this century, some of whom, like Paul Florensky, were considerable physicists, formulated a dynamic theory of matter which incorporated the basic scriptural notions of the cosmic significance of the fall, the miracles of Christ, his spiritual corporeity, the resurrection of the body and its anticipation through holiness.

For Gregory of Nyssa, for example, matter results from the convergence of intelligible structures. We must be clear that Gregory attributes a certain materiality to the intelligible, God alone being immaterial. What he means is that 'matter' is the concretion of 'thoughts' 'perceptible by the spirit and not by the senses', and that these created structures are the place where divine Intelligence and human intelligence meet. We might ask whether modern science, when it discovers 'systems' and 'structures' of amazing complexity, without which the universe could not exist, is not coming to similar conclusions.

For the Fathers and for the great ascetics – who speak from experience – this conception shows that there exist very diverse spiritual states of materiality, which, in human terms, can be understood as states of contemplation or blindness. In other words, the condition of the cosmos, its transparence or its opaqueness to the divine light, depends on the transparence or opaqueness of humanity itself. In the beginning, and again now in Christ, in the Holy Spirit, humanity, by subjecting the universe to 'futility', renders itself subject to a state of matter 'against nature'.

The Fall as a cosmic catastrophe

The Fathers, by detailed study of the Bible, have demonstrated that the Fall was a truly cosmic catastrophe, eclipsing the paradisal state with a new state of universal existence. Man, the son of God, wished to kill the divine Father and take possession of Mother Earth. 'Man,' says Maximus the Confessor, 'wished to lay hold on the things of God without God, before God and not according to God's will.' And so 'he delivered the whole of nature as a prey to death' (PG,91,1156 C).

So it is that humankind can no longer see the world as it really is, upheld by God in his glory, for the creation does not impose itself on us any more than the Creator. Instead, we see the universe in the likeness of our own decay, coloured by our covetousness and disgust, and thus we tarnish it, harden it and break it in pieces. Thus come into being the murderous categories of time, space and materiality – time that brings exhaustion and death, space that separates and imprisons, and materiality, opaque, delimited, the mirror of our spiritual death. The ravished earth becomes a tomb for Man, this Oedipus with bloodshot eyes.

Meanwhile God, being shut out from the human heart, i.e. the heart of the world, nevertheless maintains it from outside, imposing enough order to keep it from totally disintegrating, and to make history possible, and in the end salvation. By their assurance of continuity, the laws of nature witness to the universal Covenant that God made with human beings the day after the Flood, after the waters had washed over the wicked human race but had failed to dissolve away the original sin of creation: 'While the earth remains, seedtime and harvest, cold and heat, summer and winter, day and night, shall not cease' (Genesis 8.22). However, that Covenant, made not only with humanity but with 'every living creature', was henceforth to include death, a bond of exteriority and violence between human beings and the universe. Human beings are reminded of their duty in the world, but they must perform it in 'fear and trembling'; and they will kill to eat, something which had no place in the state of paradise. However, as a pledge of redemption, God reserves to himself the blood, the vital essence in which he is present, which he pervades and quickens with his Breath. The wholly good creation groans, waiting to be delivered from the forces of evil which transform its worshipful transparence into the 'wall' that from the time of Sartre has haunted the modern mind.

It is from this point of view, it seems to me, that Christians ought to think about evolution. Geological and paleontological investigations are necessarily stopped at the gates of Paradise, where life was of a different order. Science, itself a product of our fallen state, cannot go back before the Fall. What science calls 'evolution' is, in spiritual terms, the progressive objectification or externalization of the place that the first Adam had in the universe, and lost. Being no longer the 'mystical body' of Adam, the world collapses into separation and death, in which state God holds it steady, keeps it safe, and directs it towards the incarnation of Christ, the new Adam. In 1924 Teilhard de Chardin, in a short essay entitled *My Universe*, wrote this (in view of his later works, remarkably traditional) account of creation:

> From whence did the universe acquire its original stain? Is it not likely that the original multiple was born, as the Bible seems to indicate, from the disintegration of an already unified

being, the first Adam; so that, in the present period, the world
is not ascending, but climbing back towards Christ, the second
Adam? If that is the case, then this present stage of evolution
(of spirit out of matter) must have been preceded by a stage of
involution (of spirit into matter), a process, of course, not veri-
fiable by experience, since it would have taken place in another
dimension of reality.

The cosmos secretly transfigured in Christ

When the Son of God, the fullness of personal existence, becomes
the Son of the Earth, he allows himself to be contained by the
universe at one point in space and time; but in reality the universe
is contained in him. He will not use his body to possess and exploit
the world, but by his constantly eucharistic attitude, he makes it a
body of unity, flesh which is both cosmic and sacrificial. In him
the world becomes a spiritual corporeity, not dematerialized but
quickened by the Spirit. Willingly he buries his luminous corporeity in our suffering and burdensome corporeity, so that on the
Cross, and in the sudden radiant dawn of Easter, everything is
bathed in light; not only the universe, but all human effort to transform it. That is why the body and blood of Christ are not just grapes
and wheat, but bread and wine! In and around him, fallen matter
ceases to enforce its necessary consequences and constraints,
becoming once again a means of communion, a temple of celebration and meeting. In and around him, the world 'frozen' by our
fallenness melts in the fire of the Spirit and recovers its original
dynamism. In and around him, time and space are no longer
divisive, but are transformed by a dimension of resurrection.

Indeed, the first Christians saw the resurrection and glorification
of Christ as affecting the whole cosmos. The Cross becomes the new
tree of life, bringing within our grasp a risen state of existence. 'This
tree rises from earth to heaven. Immortal plant, it stands at the
centre of heaven and earth, firm support of the universe, bond of

all things, weaving the universe together... In his ascension, Christ gave life and strength to all things... as if, by the sacrifice of the Cross, the divine life had reached out and penetrated everything' (Pseudo-Chrysostom, PG,LIX,743-746). Henceforward, everything, down to the conflicting principles that modern physics must hold together as it gets nearer to the essential matter of the world, bears the stamp of the cross. Thus the world is 'sacramentally', but secretly, transformed into an offering. Although illumined by Christ, it remains fixed in opaqueness because of the opaqueness of humanity. For the cosmos to be completely free it is not enough that God has become Man; Man must become God. Christ has made us capable of receiving the Spirit, of co-operating in the coming of the Kingdom.

The Fathers explain the transfiguration that is happening in terms of the hidden and the revealed. 'The fire hidden and apparently smothered under the ashes of this world... will burst the crust of death and divinely enkindle it' (St Gregory of Nyssa, PG,XLV,708 B). And Maximus the Confessor sees a universal meaning in the episode of the Burning Bush, saying that through the communion of saints there shows forth and will show forth 'that vast and indescribable fire hidden in the essence of things as in the Bush' (PG,XCI,1148 C).

Church and cosmos

Between the first and second comings of the Lord, between the God-man and the God-universe, between the fallen and trans-figured states of being, stands the Church, as a boundary and a crossing-place. And every Christian, through communion with holy things, i.e. the eucharist, and in the communion of saints, is himself a 'living boundary', a place where death passes over into life. The cosmic history of the Church is the history of a childbirth, that of the cosmos as the glorious body of deified humankind. And the Church is the divine-human womb in which this universal body, the body of the new humankind, of new men and women, is woven: 'The whole creation has been groaning in travail together until now,' waiting for the moment of regeneration (Romans 8.22-23).

The 'mysteries' of the Church, the various aspects of the life of the Church as the sacrament of the Risen Lord, constitute the heart and the meaning of the life of the universe. Things exist only through prayers, blessings, the transformations of the Church: 'By such means, matter that was hitherto dead and senseless conveys great miracles and receives into itself the strength of God' (St Gregory of Nyssa, PG,XLVI,581 B). And the eucharistic metamorphosis is the culmination of all. St Irenaeus says that we offer the whole of nature, 'eucharistizing' it. And Cyril of Jerusalem says that in the offering, 'we make a remembrance of the heaven, of the earth, of the sea, of the sun, of the moon and of the whole creation' (*Mystagogical Catecheses*, V,6). The sap rises from the earth, the water circulates and makes fruitful, heaven is married to earth in the sun and rain, humanity toils in seedtime and harvest, the storeroom thrills with dark scent, the old grain dies in the earth and the new grain under the millstone – all so that in the end we shall have food bringing us nothing but life, that in the end the flesh of the earth may become, through our work, a chalice offered to the Spirit. And the effect is also the cause; for from this luminous centre, from this dot of matter brought into the incandescence of the glorious Body, the fire spreads even to the rocks and the stars whose substance is present in the bread and wine; the eucharist guards and sanctifies the world, gradually pervading with eternity the heart of things, and making ready the transformation of the world into eucharist.

So the Church appears as the spiritual place where we are apprenticed to the eucharistic life, where we learn what it means to be priests and kings; through the liturgy the world is revealed as transfigured in Christ, henceforth cooperating in its final metamorphosis. The Church's cosmic mission is multiplied in the world by every liturgical person humbly exercising his kingship. It is in blessing that we are blessed.

The spiritual discipline and mysticism of the early Church, which have come down to us chiefly through the Eastern tradition, amount to a veritable 'physics of the glorious body'. The body, being flooded with light, then illuminates the surrounding cosmos to which it is inseparably joined. Solovyev writes that by the act of descending to the roots of life, and crucifying the cosmic *eros* in order to transform it into a regenerating force, 'we release psycho-somatic energies which gradually take possession of our material surroundings and spiritualize them... The power of humanity's creative genius, which is both carnal and spiritual, is simply the inversion, the *direction inward* of the same creative power which, directed outwardly into nature, results in... the physical multiplication of organisms.'

There are many miracles in the history of Christianity which witness, in their radiance, and their conquest of heaviness and time and space, to this spiritualizing of the body. Around the saints the whole atmosphere of nature is pacified; near to them the wild beasts, St Isaac the Syrian says, can smell the scent of Adam's breath before the Fall...

The *contemplation of nature* therefore looms large in traditional Christian spirituality. Maximus the Confessor says we must discern the spiritual essences of beings and things 'so that we may present them to God as offerings on behalf of the creation' (*Mystagogia*, II). The universe, no longer objectified by our covetousness and blindness, will be identified with the Body of the Risen Lord. We shall understand the language of creation. 'Everything around me now seemed beautiful,' says the Russian pilgrim, '... everything was praying, everything was singing glory to God! So I realized that one could learn "the language of creation" and converse with God's creatures.'

The world then stands revealed as a church, whose altar is the 'heart-spirit' of the spiritual person, one who is motivated by cosmic charity: 'What is a charitable heart?' asks St Isaac the Syrian. 'It is a heart enflamed with love for the whole creation... Whoever possesses such a heart will be unable to think of or see a creature without his eyes filling with tears of deep compassion... Such a one will pray unceasingly... even for the reptiles, out of the infinite pity which springs from a heart which is united to God' (sentence 55).

Married love also, as we know, induces a sense of harmony with nature and a closer awareness of it. The life of the universe will be transfigured, to quote Rozanov, 'not only by hermits in black but also by those richly attired for the bridal feast', and 'in the new earth that emerges there will be flowers, those flamboyant marks of sex.'

All civilization is a continual alternation between the return to paradise – in festivals, art, or holidays amongst the wonders of nature – and work, which is the humanization of the material world into a single body belonging to all. Here also we are called to co-operate with God in saving the universe. In our transformation of nature, no less than in our understanding of it, it is our role to live the great cosmic eucharist: 'We offer to thee thine own of thine own on behalf of all and for all'. So we must now face the problem of modern technology.

The biblical revelation, foundation of technology

The real difficulty with modern technology is not technical but spiritual; what would humankind or nature need to be like, to feel at home in this 'wild revolution', as Edgar Morin called it? Left to itself, technical progress becomes the tool of the rich and powerful in their struggle for profit and mastery, while the real need, that hunger for bread and for truth to which we keep referring, is ignored. What we lack, in East and West alike, is any spiritual sense of direction which would make technology our servant rather than the arbiter of our fate. This is hardly the time, therefore, for Christians to forget contemplation and the power that it brings. The more we advance technically, the more we shall need a spiritual revolution, a 'third revolution' – corresponding to that of the individual in 1789, and of society in 1917.

As we have seen, it is only because of the biblical revelation that modern technology is possible at all. In Christ, humanity recovers its creative responsibility, the dignity of a co-worker with God. Christ has freed the universe from the corruptions of paganism and sorcery; his very incarnation has abolished the dualism which turned the body into a tomb, the earth into a place of exile. His risen body is not a dematerialized ghost; it is dense with all the flesh of the earth, and all the flesh of the earth is transfigured by it. The Resurrection destroys the world as a tomb and reveals it as eucharist.

The stupendous fact of the Incarnation, that Christ is both very God and very Man, and that he reveals to us the glorious life of the Trinity, where unity and diversity coexist without abolishing each other, has demanded of the Fathers and the councils a constantly antinomic approach, a way of reasoning by contradictions, which has remained to this day the guiding principle of research. Moreover, biblical revelation has permanently unbalanced the universe by letting loose upon it the dynamism, and the tragedy, of insatiable human liberty, determined on seeking or rejecting the living God. Ever since the call of Abraham and the cross of Jesus, there has been a restlessness in the world, a quest for the absolute, a wound of the infinite; while the world, obscurely, waits for the final catastrophe and the transfiguration of the Kingdom. Modern science and technology have sprung up in this gap, in this boundlessness born of a departure, defying the earth and the stars, for an unknown destination, of a wrestling with the angel, of a God who is not the *deus ex machina* of our ignorance and our frailty, but who makes us free by dying as a slave on the cross.

Christendom and its systems of thought

We must not forget that from its beginning Christianity came into contact with a whole range of prehistoric systems of thought, whose influence penetrated the Mediterranean world after Alexander's expedition, when Greek and Asian civilizations met; sciences of inner reality and underlying causes, animist or panpsychic beliefs about existence, in which humanity and the cosmos are at one. Indian yoga and Chinese medicine, which even threaten to undermine Marxist historical materialism, are modern examples of this type of thought.

For its part, Christianity, in the face of monistic and occult beliefs, has firmly upheld the freedom and the transcendence of the person. The ascetic achievement of the great monks was to rid the earth finally of the putrescent corpse of Pan and, having thus exorcized it, to return it to the keeping of humankind.

Even so, the wisdom of the past was not entirely discarded. Taking care to avoid black magic and any tendency to pantheism, and to reserve the freedom that belongs to God and human beings – for the scholastics said of astrology, 'the stars influence, they do not determine' – Christianity made some use of this inheritance, and even transfigured it. Among other examples we might cite the influence of astrology and alchemy in Byzantium and in the West, or the Pythagorean theories of numbers and musical intervals, which were so important for the builders of churches. Thus was Christianity able to clothe human endeavours with a symbolism which could link people with the divine intelligence through the structures of the cosmos.

It was then that the old Christian lands acquired their familiar appearance. Whereas in new countries nature is either virgin or violated, and human work in India and the traditional Far East is directed towards absorption in the cosmos, nature in the old Christian countries shows the marks of grace, almost as if it had a face, and sometimes becomes the 'image of the image', that is to say, of Man the image of God.

It is only because of the energy which pre-modern Christianity, incorporating ancient universal wisdom, was able to store up, that the discoveries and inventions of the modern West have been possible.

The great divorce

By the Middle Ages, however, with the rise of humanism and rationalism, there were already the beginnings of a breach between Christianity and a self-sufficient humanity. In Byzantium, and spreading into Franciscan Italy, there was an attempt, supported by a theology of the transfiguration of the body and the earth, to transfigure the renaissance, to divinize humanism. But this last phase of Byzantine culture, which seemed so promising, was swamped by Asian influence, while Western Christianity had other interests than the fertilizing of scientific and technical progress with divine energy. The cosmic awareness of the Renaissance was then abandoned by a Christianity – whether of the Reformation or Counter-Reformation – which had become a religion of the individual soul and morality, with no power to effect real transformation in divine-humanity. Modern rationalism has therefore developed without the guidance of the Spirit.

At the end of this process all that is left is a conventional Old Testament belief threatened by Prometheanism. Science, following in the line of the great prophets of Israel, has dealt a fatal blow to all mysticism about the impersonal universe. It achieves, and renders irreversible, the birth of the human person away from the womb of Mother Earth. The experience of interplanetary flight, although vicarious for all except a few, has succeeded in breaking the umbilical cord which attached the human race to the earth.

Today, technology has rescued human beings from the old forms of poverty but has inevitably brought about the demand for justice, for the fair distribution of its products. This desire for justice here and now is the age-old claim of Israel, the one who wrestles with God. And the Churches can do nothing other than repeat it, to 'render habitable' a planet where technical progress multiplies goods and services, but only for the privileged few, while the distress of the rest of the world increases.

On top of this, there is the increasing problem of where we ought to be going. *For Christians, the desacralization of nature by the biblical revelation can only be a stage on the way towards transfiguration.*

If we are not careful, the technical universe, left to its own devices, will damage human nature in its very depths. The abnormal growth of purely cerebral calculation; the sensual refusal, in our leisure time, to do any real thinking; the increased difficulty, while working, of 'thinking with one's hands'; the coldness of metal, the abstractness of synthetic materials, the constant noise, the invasion of images that appeal to our sniggering instincts; all conduce to a weakening of the unifying powers of the 'heart-spirit'. Today these powers must be renewed, if humanity and its cosmic environment are not to be destroyed.

Exorcism

The most authentically Christian, baptismal attitude, must be one of exorcism.

In exorcizing the determinisms of technological society we are by no means condemning the scientific research and invention which spring from it. Rather, we are trying to make them have more respect for reality. Christians must demand of science a more open-ended research, and of technology an efficiency that serves the irreducible person no less than the indispensable relationship between Man and the universe; earth, if no longer our mother, must be our lover.

The possibilities of human intelligence, where God's image is particularly concentrated, have no end, in both senses of the word: they are boundless, and there is no final point at which the image will cease to be aware of itself as an image. Engaging in scientific research, and in dialogue with scientists, Christians must testify that the human person on the one hand, and created beings on the other, are strictly inexhaustible. If the inexhaustibleness remains a secret, the scientific quest will be endless. If the inexhaustibleness is recognized, the quest might be brought to completion. Christians are faced by a science enclosed in its own mythology; they must summon it to become an open science, whose questioning they can refine.

Technology and resurrection

Exorcism cannot be separated from an inner struggle for transfiguration. This struggle is not at all a matter for scientific speculation, a philosophical theory for the consideration of the learned; it is a work of faith, which the learned can undertake, if they wish, in their inmost hearts.

In us, indeed through us, the liturgical cosmos draws near to the fallen world which we study, which is there for our use; in us and through us, the light of the Transfiguration is diffused from the atom to the nebula, the 'contemplation of nature' is extended through physical and biological research, Christ's reintegrating power turns back the forces of chaos. The problem of technical civilization is increasingly one of meaning and purpose, and meaning and purpose can come only through spiritual people. Only the people of the eucharist can bring about the integration of matter. Only the people of the icon can rescue the threatened image of the person. Only people who turn the universe into a church whose altar is their own heart can remind science and technology of the sanctity of the earth, and its entitlement to humility and respect.

Here we must return to Fedorov (the 'strange librarian' of 19th century Moscow, who would happily slip into the reader's hand, not only the book he had asked for, but any other book Fedorov thought he needed...).

He suggests that the real problem is not 'the social problem in the sense of the problem of riches and of poverty, and of universal plenty', but that 'of life and death and of the universal return to life'. So Christians are to celebrate Easter 'in their daily, earthly work'. 'The liturgy must encompass the whole of life, not only the inner life of the spirit, but the exterior, worldly life, transforming it into a work of resurrection.'

Fedorov criticized the attitude of modern technology towards nature as only seeming to be positive, while actually it is the abandonment to instinct. We seek to plunder nature for immediate gratification and remain its slaves. We are controlled by technology, whereas we ought to control it as a means to a paschal end. A truly positive relationship with the cosmos must be one of life-giving communion.

Today ecological and environmental problems force themselves on our attention. In our lifetime the earth has been raped; technological humanity must enter into a living relationship with it.

According to Fedorov, spiritual discipline should be for everyone, governing our 'common work' of scientific and technical advancement.

He also recommends the blowing up of towns, not as centres of culture but as cancerous growths. People must recover, after a period of estrangement, a sense of the sanctity of the earth and, by way of that, the love of ancestors for whom the earth is the body and who sleep in it like seeds of resurrection. Progress which is not aimed at the resurrection of all would be merely a succession of murders. Indeed, today we see the crowds in our cities awkwardly seeking any opportunity of contact with the earth and with the great works of the past; we see communities of young people rejecting, as Fedorov wished them to, the endless greed of commercial civilization; they do not reject technology, however, but subject it to the requirements of a true encounter with beings and things. Technology itself, in its most modern forms, makes it possible to blow up towns and sometimes causes it to happen. The automated factory is already setting free human energy, which for the time being we would rather leave to rot in unemployment while the third world suffers poverty. We are waiting for the prophetic will that can direct it towards lifegiving forms of work.

In his conclusion Fedorov insists that only a religion of universal resurrection can bring together in one great sacrament of life the sealed-off compartments of culture. 'In the effort to recreate the world in the incorruptible beauty which it had before the Fall, a reunited science and art will become one universal ethic, aesthetic, and technology for the regeneration of the cosmos.'

8

The Third Beauty

For many people today, remote as they are from a Christianity which seems to them just talk and moralizing, life attains a religious intensity only when they experience beauty: a song pulsating to the rhythm of the blood, struck up by an adolescent to his own guitar accompaniment; a mountain in winter, when the world is transformed by snow, and light seems to radiate gently from the earth; a face, seen in such close-up that it must belong to the television or the cinema... In that beautiful moment, the humdrumness of daily life is suspended; suspended also is the desire for the power and security that technology and science can give; all is given and all is immense, I possess no longer but I am possessed, the veil of my mind is torn in two, my whole being rejoices with intimations of the wholeness of paradise.

However, as we well know in moments of desperation, beauty has no power to save. Left to her own devices, the Beautiful Woman, the Mother of the 'kingdom of Mothers', is revealed as Melusine or a prostitute; in the Eastern tradition the biblical image of the prostitute constantly recurs, from St Isaac the Syrian to Gogol, symbolizing the nocturnal allurements of the fallen world. And life's climax, the orgasmic beauty which is the aim of our civilization, is inextricably bound up with death. It is cut off from the good, and while the good, by itself, makes for mediocrity, beauty by itself makes for madness. Hölderlin, Nietchze, Van Gogh, Antonin Artaud, all went mad after being plunged in a fire whose Name they did not know.

The winter of beauty

There have been many crises in the history of beauty, especially, if we confine ourselves to Europe, at the time when hellenistic neo-classicism was evolving into the hieratic art of the 3rd century, soon to be enlightened by Christianity; or again during the long transition from mediaeval Christendom to modern humanism. Today, however, it is a matter not of a crisis, in a succession of crises, but of a *crisis*, in the full sense of 'judgement', a virtual apocalypse in history.

In this crisis, the clearest and most 'critical' tendency, is that of disintegrative experimentation which, having asserted itself in cubism and futurism, now dominates the various kinds of non-figurative art. (While these movements have been mainly characteristic of painting, similar influences in the other arts could easily be identified). This tendency is reminiscent of a negative theology which cannot transcend negation, or a descent into hell with no resurrection to follow. Every now and then, a truly creative artist succeeds in using such an approach as a means to contemplation – Braques, Bazaine or Junec, for example – but these are exceptions. For the most part we dwell in a cosmic winter where flesh and beauty have decomposed. From appearances Cubism has extracted a geometric skeleton, but this skeleton has fallen into dust at the first obstacle. Test-drilling through the strata of the sensible world has revealed, distorted in the shadows, the 'spirits of nature', the 'elements of this world' conquered by Christ. Deeper still, materiality is reabsorbed in intelligible forms; this, the inner transparency of the cosmos, is nevertheless regarded by art (and science) as of the lowest order, even as nothingness, so it becomes what the Russian religious philosophers would call 'disaffected wisdom'. In the extreme case, matter is dematerialized. Bodily flesh, as we know it in the art of ancient Greece, and partly transfigured in mediaeval Christendom, seems to rot and fall to pieces. Boundaries are erased, solids liquefy and evaporate. Humanity blends with objects, one object with another, outlines are blurred. The limit between the me and the non-me disappears, often through the agency of machines and all the apparatus of the huge city, as if the 'elements of this world' were returning and stealthily taking possession of a techology which, although supposed to be neutral, cannot be exorcized or controlled by the spirit. So it is that in the mechanical frenzy of futurism; in the convulsive beauty of surrealism, the alchemy of the hallucinating metropolis; in *American action* painting of the 50s, which is simply the depiction of a trance... the human being is dissolved, losing at once its solidity and its stability; so that futurists and surrealists, even when they proclaim themselves to be materialists, are not so in the old sense of the word; human beings disappear, but, in their very ecstasy, matter disappears as well. 'Man,' said Marinetti, 'is no longer of any interest... He must be replaced with matter whose essence we intuitively understand. We must replace the psychology of Man, which is worn out, with an ecstatic hallucination of matter.'

The most striking general characteristic of contemporary art is its rejection of the face; even those who are aware that, after their descent into hell, there might be a resurrection, find the human face virtually impossible to portray; I think of the extraordinary Holy Faces of Manessier, those immense buds of the night which can never open out. There is a parallel in literature, where words are separated from the Word and whirl around like dry leaves in the same cosmic winter (to the delight of linguistic philosophers, who use these dry leaves to carpet the antechamber of being, but it is always the antechamber). The great works of James Joyce and Andrei Biély at the beginning of the century perfectly illustrate this. Take for example Biély's *Petersburg*, only recently, after half a century, translated into French. A room and the things in it, as in certain 'happenings', become for the hero the symbols of entirely inner events. His consciousness is detached from his body and joined to the electric lamp which is alight on the desk, and the lamp becomes 'the sun of the consciousness'. Biély, an anthroposophist, understood the deep ambiguity of a reality that is not spiritual but, as he called it, 'astral', a mysterious trace of the 'wisdom' which was created to receive the divine Wisdom but which, having fallen into disuse in a materialist age and being no longer acknowledged, has now become a kind of magic. Coming just after the First World War, Dadaism did no more than draw attention to the disintegration of the language, alienated from the Word by middle-class usage, broken up by the unbridled nihilism of the world war and the devastation of Russia by civil war, terror and famine.

These 'decrystallizing' tendencies are only signs, in the realm of beauty, of a 'decrystallization' of everything, an apocalypse within history which overthrows the old certainties of life and thought. Machinery destroys the organic ways of life and, as we have said, harshly rips the person from the shelter and protection of the earth; science dissolves the universe in an ocean of abstractions, matter disintegrates, and the threat of the 'bomb' enters history like a cancer; the poor are convulsed by wretchedness and rich by nihilism – all are so many aspects of this apocalypse. The process of disintegration in art merely reflects what is happening generally. And not only reflects, but often foreshadows; for art has shown us *in advance* the world blown apart by the bomb; just as Picasso and Kafka had described *in advance* the world of the concentration camp.

What is now required of the Christian, it seems to me, is not an attempt to recover the ancient forms of beauty, but an even greater radicalism, a creative daring that leads beyond the limits of this world, not the lower limits but the higher. Apocalypse means 'revelation'. The crisis of beauty, as we have just described it, may *also* be an attempt to penetrate beyond the fallen world, to achieve a different flesh, a spiritual bodiliness which transcends the laws of our external, mutually estranged condition; to attain, by means of this negative, and for so long disintegrative quest, to the revelation of the kingdom of pure beings around the deified human face.

The impossible synthesis

Alongside this 'critical' process, and in reaction to it, for more than a century there have been attempts to make a synthesis of beauty. For the 19th century we need only recall the operas of Wagner. As this century opened, symbolism was codified according to philosophical systems. In every country of Europe, but especially in Germany and Russia, many of the *intelligentsia* felt regret for an organic age, when the highest values were mediated to society by way of an art that was all of a piece with life, that kept it in touch with its divine roots. In the 'Russian renaissance', at the beginning of the century, people dreamed of a 'theurgic' art, by which life would be changed and divinized. Scriabin wished to write and set to music a 'mystery', in the mediaeval sense, in which all human arts and values were to be united, a mystery so powerful as to bring about in its final chords a real transfiguration of the world!

But how to find a unity in which the disintegration could be reversed and turned into the dynamism of the resurrection? The disintegrating tendency was always stronger than the power to unify; whence the attempt to impose unity by force, against experiment, even against freedom if necessary.

The 'critical' process appears to be strictly bound up with the individualism of Western society, with its social atomization, with the controlling importance of money in a free economy; indeed, money hastens the rise of instinct in art, because the instincts – especially of sex and death – are good for sales. The blind expansion of technology has finished off the disintegrating effect on social life of two world wars, so that ours is a 'secular society' where all we have in common is vulgarity – and no doubt an immense and crude longing for communion...

On the other hand, the search for wholeness, at the price of liberty if necessary, has often resulted in totalitarianism. We can see the line of descent, caricatured but real, from Wagner to Hitler. The poets of the 'Russian renaissance', longing for an art that belonged to the community, welcomed the events of 1917. They were soon enough reduced to silence, but 'social realism' and 'social control' have tried to realize, by enforcement and conformity, the urgent vision of the great Russian artists of the 19th century, who rejected art for art's sake, and regarded culture as an object of luxury; who wished to make beauty into bread for the people, by which all might be nourished. The same urgency impelled the surrealists and so many Western artists and writers in the 30s and 40s to espouse communism or join a Popular Front.

Today, in Western societies, the need for synthesis is becoming clear in three main areas: functional, occult and 'neo-revolutionary'.

Synthesis of functions is the attempt to plan the city aesthetically, in the growing certainty that human beings do not live by bread alone, but also by beauty. The attempt is typified by the researches of Wright in the United States, Barragan in Mexico and Vasarely in France, among many others. Here, nothing is ruled out, whether it is an immanence which plays with the possibilities of technology (as with Vasarely's use of computers) or a sounding of the depths of existence, which makes room for the numinous without giving it a name; for example, Luis Barragan's observation that 'all architecture which does not express serenity does not fulfil its spiritual mission' acknowledges, without being specific, the needs of a total humanity. Moreover, nothing is profane; architecture – the humanization of space – when it aims at beauty, spontaneously returns to ancient symbols. For example, the plan of the Maison de la Radio, in Paris, would be familiar to Indians as their diagram of the axis of the world.

The rise of the occult, of syncretism, has left its mark on Béjart's 'mass for our times', which borrows themes from Eastern paganism and the Dionysianism of Nietzsche; and on American psychedelic art; and the strange liturgies of the Living Theatre, inspired by oriental methods of 'enstasy', mystical eroticism and drugs. These are but a few of the attempts to lure the cold and lonely Westerner towards impersonal fusion.

Finally, student 'neo-revolutionary' movements are most interesting when their object is the transfiguration of life. They offer a
critique of a 'spectator society', where everything, beginning with
culture, becomes the object of passive consumption, but where
nothing is creatively experienced. The movements have transformed
much of Western society, especially in America, arousing a taste for
the 'East', and a need, already put into practice, for a life that is
more communal, more spontaneous, more open to beauty and to
idleness, if not to actual contemplation; as if the post-industrial West
ought henceforth to adopt some of the attitudes of ancient civilization... However, as long as it is led by people who lack spiritual
knowledge, or merely pretend to have it, this movement will remain
largely cut off from the sources of lasting creativity.

If we look at it carefully, we can see that this 'critical' process,
this quest of the body for glory, the search for synthesis, is an
unconscious image of the Church, which alone, in its liturgy, can
express a truly total, 'theurgic' art.

A world-wide Late Empire

Every culture has its spiritual origin in a cult, from which little by
little it becomes detached, until it is entirely cut off and self-contained,
even perhaps the preserve of an élite. This 'decadent' phase of its
history is often the time of its highest refinement, subtlety and
consciousness. Wholeness and spontaneity give place to a nuanced
awareness, a degree of scepticism, a tolerance of diversity, a dislike
of sharp distinctions, a readiness to see shades of grey, rather than
black and white. This is epecially true of modern Western culture,
whose extension throughout the world has been both its fulfilment
and its abolition, so that it now lacks any content beyond the simple
urge to try out and accept new things, while engaging in perpetual
self-questioning. In its decadent phase (using the term with no
pejorative intent) a culture becomes accessible in a way that simultaneously enfeebles and enriches it. This is its universal stage,

when it spreads beyond its traditional organic community. This accessibility and openness are accompanied by a certain predilection for the unknown, what Spengler called 'secondary religiosity'. Thus the decaying culture of the ancient world was like a vessel prepared to receive the Christian revelation. The sense of mystery that in Roman times was kept alive by the oriental cults, the contemplative approach of the Neoplatonists, and the Stoics' faith in universal providence, all prepared the way for the great Patristic syntheses. The alternation between expressive, naturalistic portraiture and the search for a hieratic style prepared the way for the icon. It was then that barbarism came on the scene, reminding us of the darkness of our origins; the black bull's throat is cut for the blood-baptism of Mithras, and the barbarians arrive from the forests and the steppes... However, barbarian energy alone would not have been enough to revive the anaemic beauty of the ancient world, even supposing the old moribund culture had the strength to absorb it. Another dimension altogether was necessary, that of Christianity, which, from the point of view of the ancient scholar delicately sculpting his own statue, was barbaric, but barbaric only in terms of the Spirit, not according to the earth and the blood. So Christendom came into being, bringing imperishable beauty in its wake. Just before it appeared, and set about directing and restricting freedom, there existed liberal thinkers in whom the positive qualities of barbarism and 'decadence' – the qualities as it might be of Origen and Plotinus – were combined; the single-minded strength of the one and the sharply critical awareness and fondness for debate of the other. This combination, always under tension, threatening even to break apart, accounts for the originality of Byzantium at the heart of the Christian world.

The situation today is not unlike that of the Roman Empire in its later years, but on a world-wide scale. High culture has become the privilege of an élite. Acquiring it is a complicated process, entailing initiation into spiritual realms often remote in space or time or simply in sensibility. The beauty presented by this high

culture is not to be immediately appreciated; we have to be cultur-
ally conditioned. We can certainly leaf through the 'virtual gallery',
and the mass media give us every help, but it is a spectator sport,
not a creative sharing in the very mystery of existence through a
direct experience of beauty. The structuralists, adamant that each
culture is an 'ensemble', complete in itself and discontinuous with
others, pour scorn on vain attempts at historical study. And now
the highest culture is destroying itself, and the death of God is
bringing about that of humanity. But for Christians the divine-
human Event of Christmas and Easter has put a decisive end to all
these discontinuities, permitting the establishment, through history
and beyond, of a brotherhood of the living. Through our experience
of paperbacks, of sound recordings, of artistic reproduction and
contemporary theatre (when it eschews the contemptuousness
considered essential to the revolutionary spirit) we know that a
communion does persist, albeit with some discontinuous features,
and that it might be lastingly revived, provided that the dying and
risen Christ, 'that centre where the lines converge', is not hidden
for too long. Malraux was not entirely wrong to call arts centres
the cathedrals of our age. But what future has a cathedral without
an altar? The question, although it concerns the preservation and
revival of Christian culture wherever it exists, does not seek to be
answered in ecclesiastical terms. All we need is the presence of
Christians who are creators of beauty; their hearts will be the altar.

The fruitfulness of barbarism

At the same time barbarism is increasing. In the first place, it is
spreading from the third world: negatively, as the revenge of the
revolted slaves, which is the cause of all the destructiveness of
'cultural revolutions'; and positively as the witness, whether
dionysiac or contemplative, of the irrational continents – including
France itself, at whose heart there lies a third world of the soul, the
spirit of the Celts, and that of Provence, among others...

Secondly, barbarism is increasing, with a great deal of intellectual embellishment, in those 'neo-revolutionary' circles that we have just described. People sometimes feel the lack of a primitive sense of the sacred to which they can respond with every ounce of their being.

Lastly, and perhaps most fruitfully, barbarism is increasing, not in opposition to modern society, but within it. There are two main aspects to this 'internal' barbarism that seem amenable to enrichment by beauty: that of the face and, to borrow a play on words from Edgar Morin, that of the *archè* and the Ark.

At the very moment that the face is disappearing from the art of 'culture', barbaric forms of it haunt us on every side – in close-up on the cinema and television screens, in advertisements and posters; and on the streets our last folk art, the beautification of the faces of women. The face may be mysterious, rapt in its very beauty, still unopened. Or it may be the *first beauty*, that of youth, *eros*, almost impersonal, awaiting the adventure of an encounter. Often it is the face of a child that stands out, full of the innocence of paradise, suggesting the reassuring feminine values of domestic comfort and security. Occasionally, as through a rift in the screen, there appear for an instant faces from the lands of suffering, war and famine; emaciated to a state of pure anguish, crucified faces. The most intriguing faces, those most dense with *another* secret, and the rarest, are those of the dead – such as John XXIII and Che Guevara, two deaths paradoxically acceptable in a world which seems to value nothing but the prolongation of life. The motley variety of faces in which humanity is displayed is blended into a single stream and becomes part of the vulgarized gallery of the imagination. Thus destructured and intermingled, souls are liquified; values, traditions, criteria, regional differences, are dissolved or cease to matter, being merely the object of idle curiosity or careless tolerance. But there remains a beauty that is irreducible, resistant to corrosion by this acid: the face of the human being and the longing for a world-wide communion of faces.

Faced with possible dissolution in this universalizing flux, how can we keep from searching for our own roots? When the surrounding atmosphere threatens to absorb us and disperse us abroad, we need to find a land, an *archè*, an Ark, where we can be ourselves. The modern city dweller, sensing the threat of abstraction, of being cut off from the elements, is transformed into a nomad of the empty spaces, impelled to embark on a quest for the ancient original roots of being, like those who went in search of the Holy Grail. The urge is 'neo-archaic', in the strong sense of the Greek word *archè*, meaning fundamental, primitive, ideal. The quest leads across the universe and the past. It is the quest of Noah's Ark adrift on the flood of technology and that of the Ark of the Covenant in a civilization without hope; the quest for a place of silence and beauty where the magnetic patience of generations has given a face to the stones. Here, through the mediation of a land and its history, beauty becomes the expression of a covenant with mystery. On the collective scale there are the great summer migrations in search of the sun and the sea, on whose shores stand ancient temples which, now that the 'idols' have disappeared, are simply temples of the beauty of the world. Others climb mountains, traverse forests, or explore 'caves of the earth'. On the domestic scale, there is the desire, commonplace it is true, to find a regular anchorage in a place of beauty and peace.

Jung describes in his memoirs how he furnished a tower near Lake Zurich. The tower soon became almost a mother to him; returning to it, he rediscovered himself: 'I felt that I was being reborn in the stone.' Not in order to shut himself away, but in order to commune with things: 'I saw myself in each tree, in the lapping of the waves, in the clouds, in the animals that came and went, in objects.' He prepared his own wood, lit the fire, went to the spring for water, and sat in the light of a living flame. 'Such simple tasks make people simple and to be simple is difficult indeed.' In silence and in harmony with nature, ideas both very old and very new emerge: 'Here creation and play are closely allied.'

Some, rejecting the alternation of urban grind and a more real existence, even abandon city life for good, and bring ancient villages back to life, making a modest living by supplying the 'neo-archaic' movement with necessary objects or services. Among them there are Christians, quiet harbingers of a renewal of old eremitical and communal ways of life.

The beauty of God

Western culture, having spread all over the world, has become so stretched, so cut off from the depths, that it lacks the strength to contain this great upsurge of life and enlighten it. Today it wavers between speculative high refinement and chaos. Only a renewed Christianity can open the ways of beauty.

For beauty is one of the divine Names, perhaps the most forgotten, and the seal of the Well-Beloved on creation: 'Set me as a seal upon your heart, as a seal upon your arm; for love is strong as death... Many waters cannot quench love, neither can floods drown it' (Song of Songs, 8.6-7). Of all the words for God in the Bible, the most common must be 'glory' – *chabod*: it expresses not an image but the great radiance in which the very life of God is diffused. There is nothing in existence which spontaneously glorifies God, by its being, its order, its beauty, except the human being: of the Father, through the Word, in the Spirit, whom we might call the Spirit of Beauty. God is the 'Father of lights'; he is the light of beauty which penetrates to the root of everything. By the Word, imperceptible 'matter' is defined and ordered and made perceptible. The Holy Spirit, the 'giver of life', brings everything to full maturity. The *first beauty* of paradise, of the origin, the *archè*, is still reflected in the face of a child, and the splendid vitality of young creatures. But humanity has interrupted the circulation of glory, blocked the eucharistic dimension of creation. The light has become external to us, so that things now have an aspect of gloom and horror, the elements massacre the innocents.

More and more we discover, in so many fields of contemporary art, that 'we have the power to unleash the most cannibalistic images, the obsessional monsters of carnage and fornication' (Pierre Emmanuel, *The World is Within*). Monsters of a magic beauty, for, as the Areopagite says, they turn their very desire for the absolute into a tyrannical force for evil. Man is revealed as a risk for God and the cancer of being in these images which in the end only spread 'sadness for death'. The *second beauty* is the wistful longing of the fallen angel, his glorious purple already fading, at Christ's left hand, on a mosaic at Ravenna.

The beauty to which we must bear witness can therefore only be that of the Cross, the cross of blood and the cross of light inseparably combined; it recaptures the innocence of the first beauty, but only by undergoing the test of the second. Easter is the inauguration of 'the gospel of the glory of Christ, who is the image of God'. From henceforth Glory shines from a face 'made perfect through suffering'. In the Byzantine office we pray: 'Christ, the true Light which enlighteneth and sanctifieth every man that cometh into the world; let the light of thy countenance be shewed upon us, that in it we may behold the unapproachable light'. According to St Cyril, the beauty of the Son has been 'matured in time' so that we might be 'led as by the hand towards the beauty of him who engenders it' (PG,LXVIII,1034). The beauty matured in the time of the incarnation and the passion is the beauty of the face, bloodied and revived, of him who conquered death by death; the beauty of him who descended willingly into hell, so that the depth of his humiliation is the measure of the height of his love. This beauty is secret, comprehensible only to personal freedom and love. Seen through the tears of the returning conscience, the Man of Sorrows, who has no beauty according to this world, is revealed as the Transfigured Christ. The paschal cross, where the negative quest is swallowed up in affirmative Love, opens to us the fire at the heart of things, the icon of the face. Christianity is the religion of faces. Only the Face of God in humanity enables us to discern the face of all humankind in God, to decipher, in the communion of saints, the riddle of the faces that surround us today. We can no longer witness to Christ in the Spirit without this *third beauty*. The beauty of God without humankind, which is a consuming fire, so that Moses could not even approach it from behind unless his face was covered, is not enough; nor is the beauty of humankind without God, that negative way to a dead end, by which unknowing is turned into absence and the desire for the absolute into the appetite for destruction. The beauty we need is that of Emmanuel – God with us – and the Holy Spirit – us with God.

The art of the icon

In the undivided Church principles were laid down, chiefly by a decree of the 7th Ecumenical Council, governing an art of transfiguration, the art of the icon.

The whole church, of course, its architecture, frescos and mosaics, is one enormous icon which bears the same relation to space as the unfolding of the liturgy does to time; it is 'heaven on earth', the manifestation of the divine-human where the flesh destined to die is transformed into spiritual corporeity.

The icon is not, therefore, a mere decoration, or illustration of Scripture. It forms an integral part of the liturgy and is, as Leonid Ouspensky says, 'a way of knowing God and being united to him'. *By it, beauty becomes a way to know God.*

For God not only makes himself heard; he makes himself seen; he becomes a face, and the icon par excellence is that of the Cross. 'Since the Invisible, being re-clothed with flesh, has become visible, let us depict the likeness of him who was manifested' (St John Damascene, PG,XCIV,1239). The Incarnation is the justification for the icon, and the icon displays the Incarnation. If human art is able to portray a transfigured world, it is because matter itself, which the painter uses, has been secretly sanctified by the Incarnation. 'I do not worship matter, but I worship the Creator of matter who, because of me, became matter... and, by matter, saved me' (St John Damascene, PG,XCIV,1245).

To portray Christ is also to portray the members of his Body the Church; the icon shows not only God made Man, but also Man who has become God.

The icon shows a personal presence, it suggests the true face of man, his face in eternity, that third beauty to which we are called. The icon could not do without some likeness to the original. However, while entirely rejecting subjectiveness, it does not seek a photographic objectivity; its setting is communion. All icons of Christ, for example, give the impression of a fundamental similarity. But each likeness is produced by the encounter of two persons, Christ and the iconographer, at the heart of the Church's com-munion. Christ is the same in all, but in each case he is revealed to a unique person in a unique way. Thus there is only one Holy Face, whose memory the Church, the Bride, has kept faithfully, and there are as many Holy Faces as iconographers. The human face of God is inexhaustible, always retaining towards us, as the Aereopagite says, an inaccessible quality: the face of faces and the face of the Inaccessible. 'He who has seen me has seen the Father' (John 14.9). The 7th Ecumenical Council forbade the direct portrayal of the Father, the first Person of the Trinity and origin of the Godhead. In Christ transcendence gives itself but remains for ever beyond.

What is true of the face of Christ becomes true of the face of humanity filled by the Spirit. Thus the art of the icon goes beyond the opposition, described by André Malraux, between the arts of the non-Christian East, witness to an impersonal eternity, and those of the modern West, subject to sensuality and the anxiety of the individual. It is in the inexhaustible face of the person that the art of the icon expresses the eternity not of fusion but communion.

Compare the image of Christ with that of Buddha, or even the image of a Christian saint with that of a Buddhist sage. The Christian face is fulfilled in communion, the Buddhist face is abolished in an interior state in which neither self nor others exist, but only an inexpressible nothing. In both cases the face is haloed. But the Christian face is in the light like iron in the fire, the Buddhist face is enlarged, identified with the luminous sphere of which the halo is the container. The Christian face expresses simultaneously inner peace and acceptance; the Buddhist face, with eyes closed, communes with itself.

The icon, by a concrete symbolism that preserves it from any tendency to allegory, expresses the deification of humankind and the sanctification of the universe, in other words, the truth of beings and things. The symbolic, integrated in the fullness of communion, is always at the service of the person whom it reveals.

Light in an icon does not come from an exact point, for, as we read in Revelation, the new Jerusalem 'has no need of sun or moon to shine upon it, for the glory of God is its light' (21.23). It is everywhere, without casting a shadow; or rather it is always within, everything shines with an inward sunlight. The iconographers actually call the background of the icon 'light': the symbol of God 'all in all'. Perspective is often inverted. Lines do not converge towards a 'vanishing point', the sign of fallen space which separates and imprisons, but expand in the light, 'from glory to glory'. The saints are almost always shown full face – the profile suggests the breaking of communion, the beginning of absence – coming to us from infinity, opening up this deified space.

In this setting, the face is depicted according to the greatest personal likeness, but pacified, unified, illumined by the Spirit. The lips are thin and pure, the ears reduced in size. The dominating features are the huge eyes, full of seriousness and gentleness – the sanctified human being becomes 'all regard', says St Macarius – and the large, wise forehead.

Around these faces, the animals and plants, the earth and the rock are stylized according to their spiritual nature. Abstraction here is a way of making the representation more penetrating, not less. Prehistoric cave-paintings of animals would not be out of place on an icon, nor would Bazaine's depiction of the elements, in the windows at St Séverin, done in such a way as to bring out their sacramental meaning. Here also the longing for the person which torments individualistic Western art might be fulfilled; some of the faces painted by Rembrandt at the end of his life are virtually icons.

Indeed, the art of the icon has never been limited to any particular style, not even that of the Eastern Church. Christian art in the West, not only in the Romanesque period but up to the 14th century in Italy, shares the same vision. While never itself being fixed in stereotype forms, it has kept faithful to the same profound inspiration, embodied in 'canons' setting out the meaning of the icons and what incidents and people may be depicted. This inspiration, that of the divine-human, has several times included, even provoked, the researches of humanism. We are too apt to forget that the Renaissance began with Macedonian art in the early 12th century. From Macedonia and Serbia the affirmation of the human in beauty spread to Italy, there bringing about, in the 13th century, a 'transfigured renaissance', a divine-humanism, soon to fall apart in the succeeding centuries. In the Byzantine world, the movement lasted longer, culminating in the first frescos of Mistra, and even more strikingly at Constantinople, with the tenderness and the dynamism of Kariye Camii. Then came the last invasions, which destroyed Byzantine culture and drove Orthodoxy underground. Soon afterwards Christendom was riven apart. Perhaps, as a result of the present encounter between Christians of East and West, 'divine-humanism' will be able to flourish again.

A testament of beauty

Today it is not only service that must witness to the Spirit, but art, the art that unifies us in the 'heart-spirit', in the 'eye of the heart' which sees the third beauty latent in everyone, and perceives everything to be holy. The art of being astonished that the Inaccessible

God draws near to us in all the faces and all the beauty of the world.

Then we find the courage, the confidence, to reinvent our life in the Holy Spirit. 'Blessed are the meek, for they shall inherit the earth.' They already are inheritors, for they sense in all creatures the secret presence of Christ who comes again in light. Today only a certain beauty, the third, can make known the living God, the Depth who is now a Face so that faces no longer die but shine like the sun. The beauty of the saints, the beauty of inspired works, ecclesiastical or secular, truly liturgical like the icon, or even prophetic, but always in movement. Rublev, to depict God, painted youth and beauty in the sacrificial unity of the Trinity. Dostoevsky and Bernanos showed that hell cannot satisfy the human heart. Solzhenitsyn discovered, beyond hell, the tenderness and the unshakable strength of the conscience. In the Church or on its margins, we wait, learning an 'inspired holiness', capable of conveying the beauty of God. Between the close-up which reveals nothing and the art which no longer dares to portray the human face there opens the place of the Icon.

9

Death and Celebration

Victory over death

'Christ is risen from the dead, trampling down death by death! And to those in the tombs he has given life': this is the constant theme, in the Eastern Church, of the Easter celebration, the 'feast of feasts'. 'The day of Resurrection! The Passover, the Passover of the Lord! From death to life... Christ our God has brought us over... Now, all is filled with light, heaven and earth and the places under the earth. All creation celebrates the Resurrection of Christ, on whom it is founded.'

The Resurrection signifies the victory of life in its wholeness over death and hell, and offers this victory to all. And we know that death, from the point of view of the Bible and the Fathers, is not simply the end of life, nor is hell simply a spiritual state beyond the grave. Both belong to our fallen condition, with its contradictions, its deep anxiety, the slavery that surrounds it in a world where everything is external to every other thing, and especially humanity to itself. Death and hell are fallen time, the cruel time of Baudelaire's 'Clock', the time that wears us out, turns us into machines and destroys us. Death and hell are fallen space, the space that separates and imprisons. Even the logic of this world is fallen, because it always opposes or confuses. Finally, and above all, hell, in the words of the bitter philosopher, is other people, and the hatred of me for myself which turns me and myself into strangers and rivals. And despite so much tenderness and beauty – for the world, fallen as it is, is still God's creation – there is the unavoidable separation and the riddle of nothingness. The riddle by whose alchemy every revolutionary movement, every political or cultural crusade, however necessary, ends in nothing. It is as though we were fighting for justice and well-being on board a great ship, only to discover that it is sinking.

God did not create death. He, the Living, created human beings to enjoy the fullness of life. But that could only be free participation in divine existence, for 'God alone has immortality' (1 Timothy 6.16). Death came into the world and has become an ever-present shadow because humanity turned away, and continues to turn away, from the Living God. Because we are afraid to die we hope to escape by taking refuge in a life of falsity and lies, so the power of death is extended further. Humanity boasts itself of this world, thinking to make it its kingdom, looking to the world for security while enslaving it to 'vanity', that is to say to emptiness. Humanity cannot annihilate itself because it is still created by God, animated by the divine breath. But, although it lives because of God, it does not wish to live for God; and in itself it is nothing. Its very life is a 'dead life' and its soul, after physical death, survives in a phantom half-life; the Bible knows nothing of any poetry of the 'immortality of the soul'.

Death is therefore fundamentally against nature, and there is a sense in which death is always murder since it strikes against an existence intended for eternity. Death is the perversion of freedom, conferring on nothingness a paradoxical reality, making it parasitic on being, which God created for fullness. We can therefore understand Christ's description of the devil as 'father of lies' and 'a murderer from the beginning' (John 8.44-45). Lying is to prefer one's creaturely nothingness to the Truth which is God. And murder is the intrusion of death, 'for the wages of sin is death'. Not the destruction of the creature, for God is faithful, but its condition against nature: not nothingness but monstrosity.

But God is patient, with all the patience of love. The evil that he cannot prevent, because it is born of the freedom in which his omnipotence is at once fulfilled and limited, God will use to open us to his love. Thus death, 'the wages of sin', paradoxically becomes a remedy for sin. Precisely because it is against nature, it makes us aware, if we do not run away from it, of our true condition. 'God suffered man to be swallowed by a great whale, namely the author of man's transgression, not so that he should thereby perish, but because he was designing and making ready for him a scheme of salvation achieved by the Word "according to the sign of Jonah"... so that, receiving from God unlooked-for salvation, man may rise from the dead and glorify God, repeating the words of Jonah: I cried in my distress to the Lord my God and he heard me from the belly of hell' (St Irenaeus of Lyons, *Adversus Haereses* III.21.1). So God utilizes our subjection to death to prepare, little by little, by election, by Covenant, by proving of faith – salvation now coming nearer, now withdrawing, as humanity accepts or rejects it – to prepare the most favourable conditions (the actual answer being beyond determination) for the fiat of Mary, that final acceptance which allows the dispossessed Creator to re-enter the very heart of his creation to reclaim it from within and, so to speak, recreate it.

Then – 'out of the belly of hell listen to my supplication, hear my cry' – then the cross, the cross of light; then the tomb, the life-giving tomb; then the Descent into hell, the victorious Descent, breaking down the 'dividing wall'. By his self-abasement, his degradation, his passion, his dying the death of the accursed, Christ accepts into himself all hell, all the death of the fallen world, even the terrible accusation of atheism: 'My God, my God, why hast thou forsaken me?' Think what death must have meant for the God-man, who was without any sin for which death might be the consequence or the 'wages' or the cure. We are in death. He descended there, who had been able to say, 'I am the life'. The anguish of that death, encompassing all the evil of the world, and all our deaths, is inconceivable. Consequently all suffering, all hatred, all separation, all death and all our deaths are annihilated;

or rather returned, with equal force, as faith, love, unity and life, by him, or in him, who was obedient to the Father even to death, and who, being consubstantial with the Father and the Spirit in the fullness of the Trinity, became consubstantial with us even to hell. So even our hell, even our death, are filled with light, provided only that, in the presence of so great a love, our freedom will allow itself to be moved in response. Hell and death are transformed by him who, giving himself up to them in his sovereign compassion, brings the love stronger than death into the spiritual place where hatred, pride and despair bind together the kingdom of the Separator; thus, in one movement, Christ simultaneously breaks open the tombstones and the gates of hell. 'Hell was pierced to the heart when it received him who was pierced in the side by the spear, and it was consumed by the divine fire, for the salvation of us who sing: O God our Redeemer, blessed art thou!'

'To be restored to life we needed a God incarnate and put to death' (St Gregory Nazianzen). In the face of all the accusations brought against God – or caricatures of God – by modern atheism, the only possible answer that Christians can give is the Innocent one, crucified by all the evil devised by human beings, who thus offers us resurrection.

In the Risen Christ, in his glorified body, in the very opening of his wounds, it is no longer death that reigns but the Spirit, the Breath of life. And the cross of victory and of light, which is the pattern of our baptism, can henceforth transform the most desperate situation into a death-and-resurrection, a 'passover', a crossing-point on the way to eternity.

And that is what the Church, this profoundly holy institution, is: it is the baptismal womb, the eucharistic chalice, the breach made for eternity by the Resurrection in the hellish lid of the fallen world. The Church is the Mystery of the Risen Lord, the place, and the only one, where separation is completely overcome; where paschal joy, the 'feast of feasts', the triumph over death and hell are offered to our freedom, enabling it to become creative and work

towards the final manifestation of that triumph, the final transfiguration of history and the universe. The whole Christian message,
the good news, the news of fullness is summed up in these few lines
from the sermon of St John Chrysostom, read at the end of Easter
mattins in the Byzantine rite:

'Enter then into the joy of your Master... The feast is ready, let
all share in it. The fatted calf is served, let no one go away hungry.
Let all enjoy the banquet of faith. Let no one bewail his faults again,
for forgiveness has shone forth from the tomb. Let no one fear
death, for the death of the Lord has set us free. Hell took hold of a
body, and discovered God; it took hold of the earth, and it encoun-
tered heaven... "O death, where is thy sting? O grave, where is thy
victory?" (1 Corinthians 15.55). Christ is risen and life reigns.'

Prayer for universal salvation

It is out of respect for our freedom that God allows evil to exist; it
has already been conquered, but secretly, because the Holy Spirit
wishes to regenerate us from within, by a free and faithful
response, without compulsion. What matters in the history of the
Church is her holiness, her awareness, in a world that is utterly
free, that Christ has conquered death once and for all, and that his
victory is always present in his Church.

The saints after their death, the martyrs beneath the throne of
the lamb (Revelation 6.9-11) await and make ready for the final
transformation. Origen says that Christ also waits, for the full
assembly of the universal Body of which he is the head; only then
will his glory shine forth.

Thus will come about the completion of all things, when the
Spirit of life, through the communion of saints, will manifest the
whole universe as the glorified Body of Christ. Then each person, in
giving his face to the transfigured universe, will rediscover his
flesh; flesh vibrant with all its natural sensitivity, our earthly
flesh, but bathed in the life and fullness of God, who will be 'all in all',

abolishing the separations of time and space, making possible among the risen a communion beyond anything we can now imagine.

All the complexity of our nature, shaped as it has been by the dramatic events of history, and by the ways we have used and misused our freedom; all the ambiguity, henceforth transfigured, of the 'garments of skins' will find a place in the Kingdom; in the being that was created wholly good we have used our freedom to dig holes of nothingness; but we shall discover to our amazement that they have become the wounds in Christ's hands and feet and heart, through which the divine life comes to us and will come to us for ever. And all creatures brought by our love to share in the Presence will also find a place in the new Jerusalem: such-and-such an animal or tree, the tawny plain at evening, when black bulls of the night mingle with white horses of the day, all these will be there, in the radiance of the Risen Christ. For he, while his friends were fishing, had lit a charcoal fire on the lake shore to grill fishes to share with them when they returned. John, Peter, will not the nearness and the unknowing of that face always bring back to you, in the Kingdom of God, the smell of grilled fish, the glow of the charcoal, the peace of the lake where earth embraces heaven?

Nevertheless, although the hell of our fallen state has been secretly abolished in Christ, and although God must be revealed at the Last Day as 'all in all', there remains the heartrending mystery of the 'second death' of the Revelation, the final death of the human being without love plunged into the divine love. For God will never reject anybody, his love is offered to all. But the fire of that love, as St Isaac the Syrian says, is eternal joy for those who welcome it and infernal torment for those who refuse it. Generic hell, as we might call it, may have been destroyed by Christ, but for each free individual there remains the terrible possibility of personal hell. But does this not amount to a fatal obstruction to the divine plan for that universal communion which is the only hope for the fulfilment of the person?

It is true, as we have said, that the Church condemned Origenism, the certainty that all people, even the fallen angels, will ultimately be reconciled in a 'universal restitution', an apocatastasis of both nature and persons. Such a conviction actually conflicts with the stern warnings uttered by Christ in the first three Gospels, and belittles the irreducible mystery of our freedom; in asserting that evil will eventually die of exhaustion, because God alone is infinite, Origen forgets that personal freedom, precisely because it is in the image of God, is by nature absolute.

But at the same time our 'catholic conscience', in the proper sense of 'catholic', the conscience that takes account of the whole of humanity reintegrated in Christ, cannot accept the existence of an eternal damnation without any possibility of escape.

In the West, at least since patristic times, this scruple has been rare, but it haunted the thoughts and prayers of Péguy, who had been brought by evangelical socialism to an awareness of the 'consubstantiality' of all humanity. In the East, right up to the present day, there have been souls consumed with love who have prayed for the damned, even for the devils. This attitude has not been the preserve of the spiritual-minded. Russian Christians, in particular, are much exercised for the damned, believing, for instance, that the Virgin, by her prayers, has obtained relief of their pain, each year, from Holy Thursday till Pentecost, the very liturgical season when universal Restoration is proclaimed and already begins to take effect. Is the contradiction, then, between freedom and love immpossible to resolve?

First we should notice that the early Church, all expectant for Christ's return, scarcely acknowledged the existence of any who had been damned for all eternity, any more than it acknowledged that the saints would enjoy an immediate consummation and bliss. The Fathers were more often concerned with the notion of purification and progressive healing. After death, the soul whose sanctification is incomplete must journey through the 'lower' worlds, presenting itself at symbolic 'customs posts' where the powers of evil take away what belongs to them, progressively stripping it bare, constraining it to peace and silence. The 'sleep' of death is thus portrayed as a contemplative state; death, dismantling the fallen being, offers to the soul, almost forces upon it, the peaceful, 'not-passionate' state that prayerful people experience even in this world, the peace which is the gentle visitation of Christ who is always present in hell, who, together with his saints, fills everything. For some of the dead, locked in ignorance or hostility, the early Church knew that peace, or silence, or the glimpse of the divine Doctor would be experienced as torments; but prayer was offered wholeheartedly for all the dead, especially for those making this journey through the underworld, those, in other words, who are in hell. In all the Eastern rites, at vespers for Pentecost, there are ancient 'kneeling prayers'. The Byzantine version reads: 'In this feast of fullness and salvation, thou dost graciously hear our prayers of atonement for those who are shut in hell and givest us the great hope of seeing thee grant to the departed the deliverance from the evils which condemn them...' The love of God, multiplied by the prayer of the Church, works from within – for no one is alone – upon the ultimate hell, individual solitude, to open it to the communion of the Kingdom that is coming.

As for the problem of the 'second death' and the final hell after the Last Day, a solution, existential rather than doctrinal, is to be found in the high Eastern spirituality associated with St Antony. A cobbler in Alexandria, to whom Christ had sent Antony to show him a degree of holiness greater than his own, confessed to the famous hermit that he used to think, as he watched the passers-by, 'May they all be saved! I alone deserve damnation.' And all this without despairing. This attitude has become a constant part of the Orthodox spiritual tradition; Staretz Silhouan, who died at Athos in 1938, heard Christ say to him, 'Keep thy spirit in hell, but do not despair'.

Of one thing we may be sure, that hell is not something to

speculate about, in a detached and logical way, while making the mental reservation that hell is for other people. When speaking of hell we must use only the language of I and Thou, of repentance and expectation; for, as Ambrose of Optino said in the last century, 'we are saved between fear and hope'. The warnings in the Gospel are addressed to *me*, my response to them will have momentous and eternal consequences; they drive me to profound repentance, to the awareness that I am in hell, that I am responsible for hell – and equally that, if I can keep from despairing, my humility brings me into the presence of Christ, who has conquered hell for eternity. But as for *you*, the innumerable Thou, my neighbour; I can only serve, pray, and hope that you will be saved, that Christ will so overwhelm you with his tenderness and beauty that your doubts, your hesitations, your fears will disappear to make room for the 'great joy'. Apocastasis cannot be a certainty, it must be the end to which our spiritual combat is directed. Let us pray and exercise discernment so that the fire of Judgement, which is the fire of divine love, consumes not the wicked person but the encroachments of evil within each one of us. For the Judge is also the defending Counsel, and the Cross, according to Maximus the Confessor, is the 'judgement of judgement'. Isaac of Syria says, 'A handful of sand in the vast sea, that is what the sin of all flesh is in comparison with the mercy of God' (sentence 107); and for him, true sin consists in not paying sufficient heed to the Resurrection which restores us from the bottom of hell 'to the joy of the love of Christ; what is hell in the face of the grace of his Resurrection?' (sentence 118).

Thus it was that the undivided Church rejected universal salvation as a doctrine, but adopted it as something to hope and pray for. This is the view of many of the Eastern Fathers, as well as several in the West. St Ambrose of Milan says that 'the same person is simultaneously saved and condemned' (PL,XV,1502). And what must we do to be saved? We are to remember that we are condemned but must not give up hope. We must be opened to the Paschal joy by the communion of saints.

The last word of Christianity is not hell but victory over hell; God does not promise us universal salvation because he can only offer it to us and wait for our response, our love, to let it happen.

The last word belongs to the feast.

The 'feast of feasts'

The feast is essentially beauty in profusion, life lived for enjoyment, without regard to usefulness, life free from care and responsibility. It is the sharing of friendship, living so intensely that even death seems forgotten. It is spontaneity and grace, a wholehearted yes to life, the great celebration which joins us to the infinite.

In modern Western society, the virtues of seriousness, saving up, work, and reliance on willpower have put out the fires of feasting, have invested in technological power what Georges Bataille called the 'accursed part' of each civilization, and what might equally well be called the holy part. We are defined by our reason and power, we have allowed our faculty for celebration to wither away. And there is undoubtedly a hidden link between the decline of the feast and the absence of God in a daily life that has become 'one-dimensional'.

Today we are seeing a revival of the feast. The pioneers of the revolution of May 1968 wished life to be like a feast, and their psychodramas in the Latin Quarter, the very home of a culture closed to anything that transcends the human, were evidence of a kind of liturgical longing, the liturgy being essentially life itself with its wholeness and depth restored. And new mystics are also appearing, whose mysticism is not merely individual and secret, but danced, shouted, lived together.

But the new revolutionaries wish to transfigure life while spurning the spiritual sources without which there can be no genuine transfiguration. And the new mystics too often celebrate for the sake of celebrating and risk dissolving themselves in an impersonalism unthinkingly imported from Asia. Both end by making ecstasy the end in itself, even to the extent of destroying themselves with sex and drugs.

In fact, if Christ is not risen, death will always have the last word, the days following the feast will be days of ashes and loneliness.

But if Christ is risen, Easter is the 'feast of feasts', and we are henceforth capable of 'giving thanks in all things', so that in the course of our daily struggle, even in martyrdom, we can be in a state of celebration.

The feast of the Church is closely allied to contemplation. The feast gives to each of us a first experience of the living God. It opens the 'eye of the heart' to his presence and makes us able to see for a moment the icon of the face, the fire at the heart of things. In the feast any being and any thing is revealed as a miracle, so that, around the sanctified person, the world itself enters into feasting and in the miracle recovers its original transparency.

The saint is the person consumed by the joy of Easter, the 'feast of feasts', who, like Seraphim of Sarov, can greet a neighbour with the words, 'My joy! Christ is risen!'

Then we realize that the feast in the world and the feast in the Church are rather alike, but there is a difference in order. In the world there is first exaltation, then bitterness; first the intensity of life, then sadness at the taste of death. In the Church there is first bitterness, then death to self, repentance that breaks down our insensitivity; then immense joy and peace, from having been forgiven, loved and recreated, the joy of thus being all together, so many wondering children.

Now the Paschal feast, and the feast of the eucharist which makes it present, are themselves only an anticipation – real and nutritious nevertheless – of the feast par excellence, that of the new Jerusalem. Then God himself 'will wipe away every tear from our eyes' (Revelation 21.4) and the Church's festival symbolism will be at once abolished and universalized; *the Feast will be manifested as the essence of everything*. There will no longer be any Temple, for the Lamb will illumine all things directly, and, as a prophet once said, even the saucepans will be holy. The Feast will be manifested as the very essence of human nature fulfilled in love between persons, in the image and within the attractive influence of the Trinity. In particular it will be manifested as the essence of *eros* and of nourishment, a doubly 'eucharistic' bond with the other and with the world. For the Kingdom will be a marriage supper, like that of Cana: 'Let us make merry, let us drink the wine of great gladness... And there are the bridegroom and the bride... And do you see our Sun... He became like one of us from love and he makes merry with us; changes water into wine, so as not to cut short the gladness of the guests. He is expecting new guests, he is calling new ones unceasingly and for ever and ever. And look, here comes the new wine' (Dostoevsky, *The Brothers Karamazov*).

By the same author

THE ROOTS OF CHRISTIAN MYSTICISM
Olivier Clément

Now in its Fifth Edition, *The Roots of Christian Mysticism* has proved itself a modern classic. By linking together a series of brilliantly chosen texts from the early centuries of the Church with a profound and sometimes highly poetic essay, the author lays bare the roots of the mysticism that has flourished among Christians throughout the ages.

Sometimes it comes as a surprise to recall that, in the first place, Christianity is both an oriental and a mystical religion - with all the risk of responding to the Infinite that breaks into everyday life to unite humanity to itself. Nowhere is this more clear than in the writings of the Fathers of the Church. Their experience was as vibrant as was their thought. With perception, sensitivity and academic skill, Clément illuminates the great themes so dear to their hearts.

"There are some books so good that all one wants to say is: go out, buy it and read it - it is marvellous! And so it is with this fine translation." **Andrew Louth, Fairacres Chronicle.**

380 pages paperback

UK Edition:	ISBN 0-904287-44-0	£14.95
USA Edition:	ISBN 1-56548-029-5	$19.95